M

American
Hiking
Society

Ame
Nation

Journeys acros

Glenn

FALCON®

GUILFORD, CONNECTICUT
AN IMPRINT OF THE GLOBE PEQUOT PRESS

Acknowledgments

American Hiking Society gratefully acknowledges the support and encouragement of the National Park Service and the Blue Ridge Center for Environmental Stewardship.

And we sincerely appreciate the generosity of the wonderful photographers.

A FALCON GUIDE®

Copyright © 2002 by American Hiking Society

Falcon and FalconGuide are registered trademarks of The Globe Pequot Press.

Text design and map: Lisa Reneson

Library of Congress Cataloging-in-Publication Data
Scherer, Glenn.
    America's national trails: journeys across land and time / by Glenn Scherer.
—1st ed.
    p. cm. — (A Falcon guide)
    ISBN 0-7627-2356-4
    1. United States—Guidebooks. 2. Trails—United States—Guidebooks. 3. National parks and reserves—United States—Guidebooks. 4. Hiking—United States—Guidebooks. 5. United States—Description and travel. I. Title. II. Series.
E158.S35 2002
917.304'929—dc21   2002019895

Manufactured in Korea
First edition/First printing

Table of Contents

Introduction: Our National Trails— A Work In Progress

I SPENT MORE CHILDHOOD days than I can remember on the Appalachian National Scenic Trail. My family returned again and again, always seeing or learning something new: watching the rush of a swollen Shenandoah River, or catching sight of deer or bear tracks or eating wild blackberries. As a child, I never thought about how and why the trail got there or who took care of it. I just knew that each time I returned it would open new adventures to me.

Eventually, I learned that "my" stretch of the Appalachian Trail didn't end in Harpers Ferry, West Virginia. It extended up to Maine and down to Georgia. And there were seven other national scenic trails. Like the AT, they are all protected by Congress for their significant scenic values. But each allows people to explore a different part of the country on foot. Beyond the scenic trails, there are 12 national historic trails (now 14, as of the publishing of this book). This National Trails System of 20 trails (now 22) tells the story of America. The national scenic trails reveal our desire for preserving quiet, scenic magnificent places. The national historic trails commemorate our greatest national triumphs, such as the exploration of Lewis and Clark, and our greatest tragedies: the forced exodus of the Cherokee Indians over the Trail of Tears.

Together, the stories run back at least 15,000 years, with the recession of the last Ice Age. These trails mark the bold routes of Spanish and American explorers, of hopeful emigrants seeking homes in Oregon or fortunes in California, of Mormons seeking religious freedom in Utah and of African-Americans fighting for the right to vote in Alabama. These are trails of commerce leading to Santa Fe, or the Pony Express Trail linking East Coast with West. Others preserve our fantastic natural heritage, from the mangrove swamps of Florida, to the peaks of the Sierra Nevada, to the quiet, dense forests of the Blue Ridge Mountains.

Above and beyond the history and landscapes that these trails celebrate, what fascinates me is how those trails came to be protected today. Almost none of them would have ever been built or would still exist without passionate people of vision, often private citizens. Volunteers are the life-blood of national trails. In the year 2000, volunteers spent well over a half a million hours building, maintaining, protecting and interpreting these trails.

The Appalachian Trail was built by volunteers 40 years before President Lyndon Johnson signed the National Trails System Act into law in 1968. He gave a tremendous boost to the grassroots American trails movement. Today, the truly successful national scenic and national historic trails are supported equally strongly by volunteer-based nonprofit organizations and federal and state governments. Each trail can move forward only as a true collaboration between government partners and organized citizen volunteers. This formal public-private partnership has legitimized and strengthened the trails movement.

Becoming a national trail is a rigorous process that often takes more than ten years, involving two separate bills before the U.S. Congress, a full corridor analysis by the National Park Service, Bureau of Land Management or the USDA Forest Service and private citizen input. Eventually, Congress may add other trails to these 22 national scenic and historic trails.

Not only is the system as a whole changing, but the trails themselves are organic and evolving. One way to measure our national trails is in completed miles. When using this tool, we find that many are not yet complete. But in some sense they will never be finished. The Appalachian Trail, our first national trail, required 16 years to be built, and today its route across the landscape is changed a little each year to meet the needs of the public.

The trails are presented chronologically by the stories they commemorate, from Wisconsin's glacial era 10,000 years ago to the Civil Rights march from Selma to Montgomery in 1965. This book is unfinished, because the stories of these trails are not over. Volunteers will continue to work with their federal and state partners and national organizations like American Hiking Society to preserve the resources which these trails tie together—be they vistas along the North Country National Scenic Trail or wagon ruts on the Oregon National Historic Trail—to provide future generations access to the essential stories and values for which each trail was established.

In fact, since this book was written, two additional trails have been added to the Trails System: the 404-mile El Camino Real de Tierra Adentro National Historic Trail (October, 2000) and the 175-mile Ala Kahakai National Historic Trail (November, 2000).

In this book, we present snapshots of our National Trails System. A book of this size could not possibly represent the full scope of a 40,000-mile trail network. These are picture postcards, then, that try to relate some of the passion felt by the trail community for its individual trails. Our hope is to pull them all together into a unified system of many trails, with one goal: to conserve our nation's natural and cultural heritage and to share it with all Americans and the world.

America's National Trails

Ice Age National Scenic Trail

It's Quiet, It's Slow, It's Free...

MILLIONS OF YEARS AGO, the first soft snowflake fell on what was to become Wisconsin's Bald Bluff. A blizzard of snowflakes followed, piling into an ice mountain a mile thick and covering the upper third of North America. Waves of ice scoured the land, driving back mastodons and sabertooth tigers.

Just 15,000 years ago, the ice melted, leaving sculpted Bald Bluff bare. Plants returned. Arctic tundra gave way to spruce forest, then to oak savanna. In recent centuries, Potawatomi Indians built signal fires at this high place.

Today, the bluff is protected as part of Kettle Moraine State Forest, one of many natural attractions scattered like beads along the Ice Age Trail and one of the earliest Trail segments to be built.

"My grandmother brought me for a walk on Bald Bluff when I was just three years old," says Christine Thisted. "Today, I'm director of the Ice Age Park and Trail Foundation, and I work to preserve spots like this."

Devil's Lake State Park, situated along the Ice Age Trail, in winter.

The purpose of the Ice Age Trail, as conceived by founder Ray Zillmer in the 1950s, is to tell Wisconsin's compelling geological story. The trail corridor preserves the fantastic landforms shaped by the ebb and flow of ice. The 1,200-mile trail and greenway (of which more than 500 miles are complete) takes a long looping course along the terminal moraine of the most recent continental glacier to sweep down over North America, the so-called Wisconsin Glacier.

The Trail winds among Wisconsin's forest-cloaked hills, meandering over snake-like eskers, teardrop-shaped drumlins and cone-shaped kames deposited by the retreating ice. The path runs beside water bodies born of the glacial age: kettle hole lakes, bogs, rivers and gorges etched by milky floods of meltwater.

But the geological story is only one side of the tale. "The Ice Age Trail is a wonderful place for solitude for the multitude, a way to get out into nature for the healthiest of recreational opportunities: hiking, snowshoeing and, in some places, cross-country skiing," says Henry Reuss, who introduced the federal legislation to authorize the Trail in 1980. In that same year, the Trail was designated a National Scenic Trail by Congress.

"Some people expect that the Ice Age Trail, like the Appalachian Trail, will be about wilderness. It's not. It is about community, and that's what gives our Trail its unique value," says Christine Thisted. "Wisconsin's urban and rural scenery, our villages and

As open land grows scarce and people get busier, becoming more disconnected from the land, the Ice Age Trail and other national scenic trails will be there to help people reconnect with nature.

Christine Thisted
Executive Director, Ice Age Park
and Trail Foundation

farms, show us that the effects of the glacier are still with us. The ice created beautiful places where people want to live." The Trail also links diverse ethnic groups as it cuts across the historic immigrant pathways over which German, Norwegian, Swedish and Slavic settlers passed in the 1800s.

Dick Cates, a former president of the Ice Age Park and Trail Foundation,

Fall color highlights the Ice Age National Scenic Trail.

istrator, the Wisconsin Department of Natural Resources, and the Ice Age Park and Trail Foundation. The Trail faces serious challenges to its completion, as suburban development flourishes and Wisconsin property values soar. But as Henry Reuss likes to point out, the Trail also moves like a glacier: slowly and steadily forward.

Dick Cates waves aside questions of completeness. "Building a trail is as exciting an adventure as walking one, and not to be missed. You have to scout a route, secure land agreements and build the treadway. As a volunteer, you have to convince each property owner that you care as much about the land as he or she does. You must be humble and tolerant and woo people; show and win respect."

The boundless energy of its volunteers drives the Trail forward. "They're a family, with all eyes set on the same goal." Christine Thisted says. "Everyone has a seat at the table and something to offer: Boy Scouts, youth at risk, seniors, homemakers, heads of corporations. We have two physicists who do controlled burns on prairies, and a 79-year-old retired lumberjack who is our best land negotiator. One and all, they love the tangible results they see as the Trail grows mile by mile."

sees the greenway as a way to find meaning in modern times. "When you step onto the Trail, you shed yourself, like a snake sheds its skin. You think about who you are, what you want to be. It's quiet, it's slow, and it's free." Cates also values the lively community of the Trail. "As you hike you might meet a guy who knows all about spiders, a woman who loves wildflowers, an amateur geologist-detective searching for clues of how the glacier formed and flowed."

Today, the Ice Age Trail is being created and maintained through a three-way partnership between the National Park Service as federal admin-

Trails for All Americans

The National Trails System—a 40,000-mile trail network—is as varied as the landscape and people of America. It was created by the National Trails System Act of 1968.

The Act named the Appalachian Trail and Pacific Crest Trail as the country's first two national scenic trails. As importantly, it created a way for Americans to add new trails to the system in several categories:

National Scenic Trails: These continuous long-distance pathways offer outdoor recreation within protected natural corridors. Some are reserved exclusively for foot travel, while others invite equestrian and other non-motorized uses. All protect natural and cultural resources while allowing visitors to experience scenic beauty and solitude.

National Historic Trails: These pathways (a category added in 1978) recognize significant past routes of exploration and discovery, westward migration and military action. They are not necessarily continuous trails. They include marked historic segments, auto routes, interpretive sites, museums and wayside exhibits.

National Recreation Trails: These existing trails offer a variety of recreational experiences and are recognized as part of the National Trails System by the Secretaries of the Interior and Agriculture Departments. They can cover hundreds of miles or be less than a mile long. There are some 800 totaling about 9,000 miles in length.

Side and Connecting Trails: These pathways provide additional access to and between components of the National Trails System. Only two have been recognized, both in 1990.

"We've gone from baby steps to big steps," Dick Cates says. "Once upon a time you could stop a hundred people on the street, and not one would have heard of the Ice Age Trail. That's all changed. We have public support, a strong volunteer base and strong partners in the Wisconsin Department of Natural Resources and National Park Service. But of course, there's just one way to build a community: that's one person at a time. It's great fun."

Juan Bautista de Anza National Historic Trail

Celebrating America's Spanish Heritage in the Fast-Changing West

IN 1976 AND AGAIN IN 1996, citizens of two modern nations were treated to an unusual sight. A Spanish soldier in a tri-cornered hat rode a white horse north for 1,800 miles, from Mexico to San Francisco. For part of the way, a retinue of 18th century Spanish *soldados de cuera,* carrying nine-foot lances, accompanied him across deserts and down urban streets.

This entourage was welcomed by public officials reading proclamations, by cheering school children, by priests giving blessings at old Spanish missions and by American Indians, who smudged the riders' foreheads with ash and offered prayers.

The riders commemorated significant events of 1775–1776. In those years, Juan Bautista de Anza led 198 Mexican recruits and their families—a third of them under the age of 12—

The 1976 Bicentennial Reenactment leaving Santa Barbara, California, on its way to San Francisco.

Top left: Desert—Maricopa County, Arizona; Top right: Oak Savanna—Alameda County, California; Bottom right: Ocean—Santa Barbara County, California; Bottom left: River—Los Angeles River, California.

across vast stretches of desert to colonize northern California for Spain.

The settlers—provided with new clothes, supplies, a thousand head of livestock and the promise of land by the Viceroy of New Spain—endured rain, snow, sandstorms, lack of water, desert sun and desert snow, even an earthquake. Remarkably, they achieved their destination stronger than when they started; only one died, while several babies were born on the arduous trip.

"Relegated as a footnote to history for 200 years, it's time we recognized the impact of Anza's expedition on history," declares George Cardinet, the father of the Trail and founder of its nonprofit support group, the Amigos

de Anza. "The expedition gave validity to Spain's claim to the San Francisco Bay Area, kept the Russians and English out and established a land route from south to north."

The rebirth of the Trail came in 1976, America's Bicentennial year. That's when history buff Cardinet and others launched the first commemorative ride. "After sitting astride a horse all the way from Mexico to San Francisco, it just seemed a shame to let it all end there," Cardinet laughs. "So we got California Senator Cranston to examine the possibility of designating Anza as a National Historic Trail, which is exactly what happened in 1990."

Equestrians enjoy the Anza Trail in Anza Borrego Desert State Park. ©National Park Service

Today, two national park units anchor the ends of the Trail in the United States. Tumacacori National Historical Park (a Trail stop near the Mexico-Arizona border) marks the south end, while the Presidio in San Francisco (a fort built by the settlers to protect their claim to the Bay Area) anchors the north. Varied landscapes and dozens of expedition landmarks lie between.

"A person traveling the Trail today will see many places essentially

When I fly over the desert by jet and imagine my ancestors finding their way below by horse, I wonder what unimaginable changes we'll see in the next 200 years.

Peter Cole, Anza expedition descendant

unchanged and some completely transformed," says Raymond Murray, National Park Service Planning and Partnerships Team Leader for the Pacific Great Basin Support Office. "The Trail lets you step back in time in the desert at Tumacacori, but it also goes down the middle of the El Camino Real, past shopping centers near San Francisco International Airport. The only lasting resonance found on some landscapes is the Spanish place names."

Cardinet points to another echo of Anza's expedition. "The woods are full of expedition descendants. You can go through the San Francisco phone book and pick out their names, though many don't even know that they're descendants."

Peter Cole is a proud expedition descendant who appreciates the Trail's significance. "I rode in the 1996 reenactment because I wanted to see where my Spanish ancestors climbed on their horses in Mexico, where they forded rivers and where my ancestor Maria Martina de Castro had her baby while coming north."

The Trail honors still another ethnic group. "Anza was significantly helped by American Indian tribes, such as the Quechan ('Yuma' to the Spanish). That Arizona tribe fed the entire party," remarks Meredith Kaplan, National Park Service Superintendent for the Juan Bautista de Anza National Historic Trail. "While the expedition's passage didn't have a big effect on local tribes, the course of Spanish-Mexican

The Trail Maker's Toolbox

Necessity is said to be the mother of invention. And when it comes to trails, lack of funding has resulted in a profound wealth of innovation.

Only the Appalachian Trail has been fully funded by the federal government to protect its entire length. For most other national trails, federal land purchase is not currently an option. Congress has even forbidden the use of federal dollars and public condemnation for land acquisition along many of the national trails.

Private land trusts, like the one established by the Ice Age Trail, are one way around funding shortfalls. Trusts seek out land and monetary donations with which to secure corridors. Matching agreements between state, county and municipal partners aid in funding. Conservation easements or leases, negotiated with private land holders, are another way to protect corridors.

On National Historic Trails, voluntary site and segment certification agreements made with private land holders are an invaluable preservation tool. These non-binding, good-faith, written agreements try to preserve natural and cultural resources and assure public access, while respecting the land owner's need to use the land, protect privacy and property.

Time has shown the certification process to be effective, even after the transfer of land from one owner to the next. "What we do not understand, we neglect, waste and fear," notes the Association of Interpretive Naturalists. "What we understand, we value, we protect and cultivate."

colonization had a huge impact. Today, we've approached the California and Arizona tribes along the route, and we're getting their advice on Trail interpretation. They want people to know that their culture is still strong today, and that they're still here."

"Of course, our challenge is to build all of these public-private partnerships quickly, before development pressures erase all traces of the Trail," says Raymond Murray. "Through these partnerships we have the opportunity to celebrate, commemorate and dedicate our heritage."

When complete, the Juan Bautista de Anza National Historic Trail will include a marked auto-tour route with more than 100 stops, plus many opportunities for hiking, horseback riding and bicycling. With 1,200 miles of Trail in the U.S. and 600 in Mexico, the potential for an international historic trail is also very real. "The Anza Trail is a window into our past," says Meredith Kaplan. "It offers an opportunity to teach people that our country was not only settled from the east by the U.S., but by the Spanish from south to north."

Overmountain Victory National Historic Trail

Revolutionary War Turning Point

PATRIOT ROBERT SEVIER'S Revolutionary War service ended on a pine- and poplar-covered knoll in the southern Appalachian Mountains. Here the 23-year-old captain died of wounds received at the Battle of Kings Mountain and was laid to rest by his buckskinned comrades.

Only a few weeks before, Sevier and 900 untrained backwoods militiamen left home, marched 225 miles in 14 days and soundly thrashed the Loyalist troops of Major Patrick Ferguson. After five dreary and indecisive years of war, the Overmountain Men had rescued the southern colonies from the British and irreversibly turned the tide of battle, leading to a final American victory at Yorktown just a year later in 1781.

The Sevier gravesite has stayed largely unchanged for more than 200 years. Trees have grown tall, and birds sing in the branches. Recently, local Boy Scouts encircled the spot with a zigzag rail fence. Every autumn for the past 25 years, reenactors of the Overmountain Victory Trail Association (OVTA) have returned to this spot to fire a 28-gun salute—each volley offered in honor of one of the patriot dead at Kings Mountain.

© SAM LLOYD

© SAM LLOYD

"It always seems to be raining when we arrive," says Mike Dahl, vice president of the nonprofit OVTA and a regular participant in annual Overmountain Victory National Historic Trail reenactments. "Mist hangs in the air and water drips from the pines. No one speaks. There's a reverence here that makes you tread softer and listen closer."

It was this same sense of awed respect that brought together Tom Gray and a few other grassroots organizers in 1975. They formed the OVTA, launched the first Overmountain reenactment and pushed to establish a "citizens' trail honoring a citizen army." Tennessee recognized the route over which the Overmountain men marched as a state scenic trail in 1976. The U.S. Congress designated the Overmountain Victory National Historic Trail in 1980, on the 200th anniversary of the Battle of Kings Mountain.

"Interpreting the story is central to our Trail," declares Dahl. "It embodies a pivotal moment in American history when common people, with absolutely no support from government, did an extraordinary thing. Ferguson had threatened to cross the mountains and 'lay waste the country with fire and sword' unless these frontier farmers

> [The Battle of Kings Mountain was] the turn of the tide of success.
>
> *Thomas Jefferson*

pledged British allegiance. The fiercely independent Overmountain men rose up and punished the King's arrogance."

Today, all but 40 miles of the original Overmountain Victory Trail are on paved roads. The National Park Service, in partnership with the OVTA, is marking both a continuous

First Person Accounts, Journals, Diaries and Trail Registers

"Our job as volunteers is to make sure the story of our Trail never dies," says Mike Dahl, past president of the Overmountain Victory Trail Association. One way of keeping those stories vibrant is through the preservation of first-person accounts told along each trail.

Surprisingly, the 19th century journals of Lewis and Clark, the diaries of Oregon Trail pioneers and register entries of modern Pacific Crest Trail thru-hikers share timeless similarities. They tell of remarkable sights seen, of hardship and inspiration met and of joy at trail's end.

> "I determined to encamp on the bank of the Yellow stone river . . . the whole face of the country was covered with herds of Buffaloe, Elk & Antelopes."
>
> —Meriwether Lewis; April 25, 1805

> "At last, towards evening, the old familiar black heads of thunder-clouds rose fast above the horizon, and the same deep muttering of distant thunder that had become the ordinary accompaniment of our afternoon's journey began to roll hoarsely over the prairie."
>
> —Francis Parkman; on the Oregon Trail, 1846

> "I didn't know whether to laugh or cry when I got to the last blaze—so I did both."
>
> — Steve Bruce, Appalachian Trail thru-hiker on reaching Mount Katahdin, 1991

auto-tour route and historic route.

Significant cultural sites are protected from development through certification agreements between the NPS and private landowners, state or local governments or nonprofit organizations. Nine landowners in North Carolina, for example, recently agreed to certify a 205-acre OVNHT campsite when threatened by a proposed highway. The Sevier grave, too, is on private land. It is owned by the Unimin Corporation, which has agreed to protect the site and open it to the public each year during the reenactment.

The annual reenactment attracts participants from across America. Reenactors—dressed in authentic homespun, carrying long rifles and tomahawks—march the entire Trail, while participants in modern dress hike along and camp or drive the route. Communities are treated to lively historical demonstrations. School children line up to take the patriot's

Reenactment along the Overmountain Victory Trail.

oath administered in 1780 at the Sycamore Shoals mustering site by Colonel John Sevier (future first governor of Tennessee and brother to Robert).

"The Overmountain Victory Trail begins by being about history, but it benefits the public in other significant ways," says former OVTA President R.G. Absher. "Along the modern Trail are historical sites and museums that attract tourists, plus recreational greenways that invite hikers and bicyclists. The public visiting the Trail also patronizes restaurants, gas stations and motels. Municipalities become willing partners when they see the Trail's economic value." Plans are moving forward to establish an off-road 32-mile multi-use trail link between Cowpens National Battlefield and Kings Mountain National Military Park.

Absher laments insufficient federal funding for his Trail but points to widening successful partnerships with local communities, the Daughters of the American Revolution, Boy Scouts and historical societies. Such alliances

are attempting to convert the 19th century Wilkesboro courthouse into a historical museum and to establish the Yadkin Greenway with its parallel hiking and biking trails and its Overmountain Victory Trail interpretive waysides. "Our Trail offers recreational and economic opportunities, while also protecting natural and cultural resources," Absher asserts.

"Congress can designate a National Historic Trail, but it takes passionate volunteers to breathe life into it. Otherwise the Trail is just a line on a map," Mike Dahl adds. "The National Park Service has done an extraordinary job of putting the Overmountain Victory Trail on the ground. Our role as volunteers is to make sure the story never dies. When the public joins us on the Trail and stands quietly beside us at Robert Sevier's grave, we want them to look back over their shoulders and expect to see an Overmountain man giving them the nod. You know, if you look and listen hard enough, they're still there."

Potomac Heritage
National Scenic Trail

Tracing the History of the Nation

TWO ENGINEERING wonders illustrate the dynamic natural and cultural contrasts preserved by the Potomac Heritage National Scenic Trail: the red brick archway of the Paw Paw Tunnel and the tightly woven stick-and-mud lodges of the American beaver, both landmarks of the Chesapeake and Ohio Canal.

In the 19th century, our nation's tireless drive toward commercial expansion prompted the blasting of the 3,188-foot Canal tunnel but also pushed the beaver to the brink of extinction. Today, placid waters offer solace and a sense of history to hikers, bikers, paddlers and equestrians, while providing haven to beaver, pileated woodpecker and Virginia bluebell.

"The Potomac Heritage Trail is unique among all of our national trails," states David Lillard, former president of American Hiking Society, a nonprofit partner. "It is the only

The Shenandoah River joins the Potomac River beyond the rooftops of Harpers Ferry, WV.

national scenic trail to focus on the connection between two great rivers and to pass through a major urban area. It's also the only one to have 'heritage' in its name—a scenic pathway through American history." More than a hundred national historic landmarks pepper the lush river valley, existing in a denser concentration than almost anywhere in the nation.

It is appropriate that a trail as historically rich as this be the vision of an American president. Lyndon Johnson, recalling quiet moments spent driving along the Potomac River with his wife, Lady Bird, proposed the Potomac Heritage Trail in 1965. Congress gave the idea National Scenic Trail status in 1983.

Today, the PHNST is part fact, part dream. Three trails are "official" segments: the 17-mile Mount Vernon Trail, along part of the northern Virginia shoreline; the 184.5-mile Chesapeake and Ohio Canal Towpath, which follows the north bank of the Potomac from Georgetown

The Potomac Heritage Trail joins the Mount Vernon Trail at Roosevelt Island.

in the District of Columbia to Cumberland, Maryland; and the 70-mile Laurel Highlands Hiking Trail, which climbs out of the Youghiogheny River valley at Ohiopyle, Pennsylvania, to follow Laurel Ridge. Trail segments are in the planning and development stages between Washington and the Chesapeake Bay in the counties north and south of the Potomac River and, as a rail-trail, between Cumberland and Ohiopyle.

As both a continuous route and a

In the moment of their junction, (the Shenandoah and Potomac Rivers) rush together against the mountain, render it asunder and pass off to the sea. This scene is worth a voyage across the Atlantic.

Thomas Jefferson

Canoeing provides superb access to the Potomac River shoreline.

network, the Trail will not only link significant historical sites, but natural areas and modern communities, providing recreational and educational opportunities to hikers, bicyclists, equestrians, campers, nature lovers and boaters. The Trail experience will include tidewater marshes visited by wintering bald eagles, the colonial plantations of patriots George Washington and George Mason and the termini of the former C & O Canal.

The basin's landscape is both physically and spiritually a national landscape, filled with national memories and meanings.

The Nation's River,
Dept. of Interior Report, 1968

"We cannot predict the shape or final routes—that task is being decided by local and state governments, citizens' groups and regional nonprofit organizations. The result will be a legacy for future generations," says Donald Briggs, National Park Service superintendant for the PHNST. He adds that the Trail will likely never be a continuous footpath like the Appalachian Trail. "The concept is best described as a network of trails, complemented by educational opportunities, in a 425-mile corridor." It may even include a water trail component between Cumberland and the mouth of the Potomac.

To date, the Potomac Heritage Trail has received minimal federal funding. Still, the PHNST serves as a catalyst for cooperation, bringing together many partners to define routes and the Trail experience. The Park Service offers some technical and financial support and coordination among many partner groups, which include municipal, county and state planners; historical societies; museums and historical parks; nature preserves; and hiking and biking clubs. Even the U.S. Army is a prominent partner with a planned Trail segment in Fort Belvoir.

Over the past several years, people from Washington, D.C., Maryland, Virginia and the Alleghenies have contributed substantially to the concept of a PHNST. South of Washington, volunteers and county planning staff are developing an on-road bicycle route in southern Prince George's County; on the Northern Neck of Virginia, four counties have developed a Heritage Tour for bicyclists along existing roads

and are planning a water trail. Prince William, Fairfax, Arlington, Alexandria and Loudoun county and city governments in Virginia are developing detailed studies for hiking, equestrian and bicycling trails. Out of a group convened by the Potomac Heritage Partnership, a regional nonprofit organization, the Potomac Trail Council was recently established to encourage the conservation of natural corridors and trails in the Potomac corridor.

"You need a big imagination to conceive a national trail," says David Lillard. "To us, preserving the cultural and natural landscape along the river is far more important than just connecting the dots. The river is already there to guide us. It needs to be protected and cherished."

Natchez Trace National Scenic Trail

Early American Wilderness Road

AT ROCKY SPRINGS, Mississippi—Milepost 54.8 on the Natchez Trace Parkway—hikers don day packs and stroll into deep woods. The sunken walls of the old Natchez Trace quickly rise up to meet them.

Magnolia trees, with fragrant white blossoms, and live oaks, their dense crowns dripping with Spanish moss, displace bright sun with green shade. Road noise dissipates, replaced by a hushed silence interrupted only by abrupt bursts of bird song. In a short distance, hikers can pause as the Natchez Trace bridges a little stream that languidly flows crystal clear over a gravel bed.

"You get a mysterious feeling of what this Trail was like when our country was young," says Jimmy Hodo, who roamed these southern forests as a child. "If you're possessed

> Of all the national scenic trails, this one may have the deepest historical roots.
>
> *Jimmy Hodo, Secretary, Natchez Trace Trail Conference*

by a little theatrical bent, it's easy to project yourself back in time and imagine gangs of thieves lurking behind these trees, waiting to pounce on unwary travelers." Jimmy Hodo grew up thinking that the Natchez Trace belonged to himself and the people of Mississippi. Now, as Natchez Trace Trail Conference secretary, he sees it as a wilderness road belonging to all America.

"The Natchez Trace has a long memory. It was an Indian path first and then a mercantile trail," Hodo explains. The Choctaw and Cherokee tribes blazed the way first. Spanish explorer Hernando DeSoto camped near the Trace in 1540. By 1785, frontier farmers floated their crops down river to market at New Orleans, but strong river currents prevented a water journey home. Instead, the trip back for these "Kaintucks" was afoot or on horseback along the Natchez Trace.

Local American Indians and settlers serviced the travelers, building 20 inns called "stands" and operating ferries. Meriwether Lewis (of Lewis and Clark Expedition fame) died of gunshot wounds at Grinder's stand in 1809, and suspicious circumstances surrounding his demise spawn conspiracy theories to this day.

By 1810, more than 10,000 boatmen were annually walking or riding the Trail. But just two years later, steamboat whistles on the Mississippi signaled the end of Trace commerce; it subsided into history as a peaceful forest lane.

The Trail today provides a lyrical dance between natural and historic scenery. The 445-mile Natchez Trace Parkway (authorized by Congress in 1938 as a unit of the National Park System) affords a beautiful slow drive that approximates the route of the old Trace between Natchez, Mississippi, and Nashville, Tennessee. Intertwining with the parkway is the Natchez Trace National Scenic Trail (designated by Congress in 1983), a proposed 694-mile hiking and horseback trail, of which 62 miles are complete.

The parkway and trail offer visitors a varied pallet of American history. Stops along the way include a restored Chickasaw village, American Indian ceremonial burial mounds (one dating back 2,000 years), two Civil War battlefields, the remains of U.S. Army posts, ironworks, mines, ferries and "stands." The Trace is also dotted by

Old Natchez Trace, the original pathway used c. 1790–1820. ©JIMMY HODO

modern trailheads, campgrounds and picnic groves. Its cypress swamps, oak forest, open meadow and southern pine hills resonate with evocative place names: Baker Bluff, Jackson Falls, Pigeon Roost, Witch Dance, Yockanookany and Donivan Slough.

The Natchez Trace National Scenic Trail, unlike most other national trails, was not born from a grassroots push but was created by act of Congress. It

Pearls on a String

National trails pose unique management challenges. They are sometimes only a few feet wide—yet often more than a thousand miles long—interconnecting federal lands; state, county and municipal parks; Native American tribal lands; and corporate and individually held private property.

Unlike national parks and forests, trails have no centers and no entry stations. While they are sometimes sought out as destinations by travelers, they may frequently be discovered by "accidental tourists" who stumble across them in their journeys.

As such, these linear parks require a sophisticated management system. Since limited funding makes adequate professional staffing impossible, local partners voluntarily agree to serve as trail law enforcers, maintainers, monitors, educators and interpreters. State agencies often also play key roles in corridor protection, funding, promotion and coordination.

The cornerstones of these complex cooperative partnerships are Memoranda of Understanding (MOUs) and cooperative agreements. Each trail has both—MOUs, which pledge cooperation and define roles and desired mutual outcomes; and cooperative agreements, which offer financial and technical assistance for public benefit.

These agreements are signed by the lead government agency and by its managing volunteer associations, as well as by a vast web of local cooperative partners who share responsibility for protecting and administering each trail corridor.

The Appalachian National Scenic Trail's agreements provide a typical example of the scope of these partnerships. Usually initiated by the National Park Service as the Trail's administrator, these agreements involve the Appalachian Trail Conference and its 31 volunteer maintaining clubs, the various federal parks, forests, and wildlife refuges along the Trail, state governments and even municipal watersheds. Remarkably, it is a system that works!

wasn't until 1989 that three men—Hillary Wright, Chester Null and Harold Draper—came together to form a volunteer group to carry forward the building of the footpath. "We saw it as a great opportunity to put a national trail in our backyards," relates Hillary Wright, Natchez Trace Trail Conference president. "This was a place for seniors and scouts, for everyone, to get out and enjoy nature."

Both Jimmy Hodo and Hillary Wright are active Boy Scout leaders, and it is the Scouts and horseback riding clubs who have taken up the challenge to construct much of the scenic trail so far. "We had one troop that bicycled up from Alabama to build a bridge," Wright relates. "Remember, these are not small construction projects. The bridges we build not only need to hold the weight of hikers but of horses." The National Park Service has proved itself a vital partner, sup-

Volunteers play a large role in building bridges and maintaining the Trail.

porting trail builders with materials and technical know-how.

"The Natchez Trace Trail offers a remarkably democratic experience for hikers and trail builders," says Hodo. "On a given weekend you'll meet walkers of every ethnicity, income bracket, age and background. Likewise, volunteers are welders and bankers, teachers and government employees. Whoever knows the most about bridge building or trail construction is in charge that day!"

Jimmy Hodo is proud of the contribution he and others have made to the Trail. "I feel a part of something bigger than myself. I'm on the ground floor of a project that we'll leave as a legacy to the next generation." Hodo personally doubts that the Natchez Trace Trail will ever run for 694 continuous miles. Suburbia, highways and impenetrable swamps block the way. "This will always be a day-hiker experience, a place to go slow and commune with history."

Lewis and Clark National Historic Trail

Journey with the Corps of Discovery

ON AUGUST 12, 1805, three white men climbed into Lemhi Pass, a windy gap on America's Continental Divide. They grasped the immense significance of the terrain as they stepped west out of the Louisiana Purchase.

"The road took us to the most distant fountain of the waters of the Mighty Missouri in surch of which we have spent so many toilsome days and wristless nights," wrote Meriwether Lewis in his journal. "We proceeded on to the top of the dividing ridge from which I discovered immence ranges of high mountains still to the West of us with their tops partially covered with snow. I now descended the mountains to a handsome bold runing Creek of cold Clear water. Here I first tasted the water of the great Columbia River."

American Indians had probably routinely crossed this pass for thousands of years before Lewis and Clark arrived there late that summer. But the passage of the Corps of Discovery signaled a major milestone. After them would come a trickle, then a flood, of fur trappers, adventurers, prospectors, settlers, soldiers, ranchers, railroaders and road builders, transforming the continent.

Surprisingly, Lemhi Pass is much as it was then, lonely and wild, still portioning water east and west toward two oceans but with one major difference. It annually attracts pilgrims following in the footsteps of Lewis and Clark.

Since its designation as a National Historic Trail by Congress in 1978, the Lewis and Clark Trail has drawn a growing number of visitors to its "long thin museum." Today's travelers relive the epic adventure via trail markers, signs, wayside exhibits, interpretive centers and living history sites that dot the Trail's 4,000-plus miles.

"After all, none of us can do what Christopher Columbus or Neil Armstrong did, but we can do what Lewis and Clark did—albeit in a mini van!" quips David Borlaug, former president of the Lewis and Clark Trail Heritage Foundation.

The Trail's modern auto-tour route, water trails, and hiking/horseback seg-

ments retrace the journey of the Corps of Discovery. The way west begins at the confluence of the Mississippi and Missouri Rivers where Lewis and Clark launched their keelboat and two smaller craft on May 14, 1804, as they "proceeded on under a jentle brease up the Missourie."

The Trail follows a meandering water course through the Great Plains along the sweeping bends of the river, then climbs precipitously on a land route through the folded maze of the Bitterroot Mountains. It then descends along the Clearwater, Snake and Columbia Rivers, before finally reaching the Pacific. "Great joy in camp we are in View of the Ocian," writes Clark on November 7, 1805, "this great Pacific Ocean which we been So long anxious to See."

The Expedition itself boasted a mix of at least four ethnic groups, including the 16-year-old American Indian, Sacagawea; her French-Canadian husband Toussaint Charbonneau; plus William Clark's black slave, York. The group also relied heavily on native peoples for help: the Mandan, Hidatsa, Arikara, Shoshone, Nez Perce and other tribes contributed directions, food, shelter, horses and safe passage.

"We can look back and see this as Camelot," says Borlaug, "a shining moment when Native Americans and whites got along. Today, we want to rekindle and recapture that spirit of cooperation between cultures."

With the approach of the Lewis and Clark Bicentennial Commemoration in 2004–2006, the compelling story of the Corps of Discovery is being retold

Reconstructed Fort Clatsop hauntingly evokes the Corps' damp winter of 1805–06.

with renewed energy at places like Fort Mandan, North Dakota, winter

In reality, Lewis and Clark didn't discover anything. They traversed an area as large as Europe that was already inhabited by as many diverse cultures.

David Borlaug, former President, Lewis and Clark Trail Heritage Foundation

quarters for Lewis and Clark in 1804–1805.

"We've made a real commitment to the accurate portrayal of frontier life here," says Borlaug. "Eventually, we hope to see the Fort become a 'Little Williamsburg.' People will see the depressions in the ground where Mandan lodges stood. Better yet,

they'll meet Mandan descendants."

The Bicentennial is likely to offer an economic boon to state and local economies. Washburn, North Dakota, for example—site of Fort Mandan and home to just 1,400 residents—is already annually entertaining 25,000 visitors. The Lewis and Clark Trail is preparing for the influx of travelers. Administered by the National Park Service, the Trail has strong active partners in the Lewis and Clark Trail Heritage Foundation, National Council for the Lewis and Clark Bicentennial, many other federal agencies, state and local governments, American Indian tribes, private property owners and others.

David Nicandri, former president of the National Lewis and Clark Bicentennial Council, defines the

Protecting Natural and Cultural Resources

When Thomas Jefferson sent Lewis and Clark west, he authorized what may have been America's first natural and cultural resource survey: "You will," said Jefferson, "endeavor to make yourself acquainted with names of the nations and their numbers; their language, traditions, arts and customs… [An]other object worthy of notice will be the soil, the face of the country, its growth and vegetable productions; the animals of the country…"

Today's land managers continue to struggle with the seemingly insurmountable charter of inventorying, monitoring and protecting natural and cultural resources associated with national trail corridors.

At Fort Clatsop National Memorial, Lewis and Clark's 1805–06 winter quarters in Oregon, caretakers not only have restored the fort itself, but try to preserve the spruce-hemlock-cedar forests and sedge-cattail tidal wetlands that helped ensure the survival of the expedition. "As a consequence, these natural components . . . are managed as a historic as well as a natural resource," writes Cynthia Orlando, the Memorial's former superintendent.

Similarly, the fertile soils, moraines and drumlins deposited by glaciers also determined early settlement and farming patterns in Wisconsin— becoming a key natural and cultural component of the Ice Age National Scenic Trail's story line.

In the next century, national trail managers will struggle to protect natural and cultural resources against mounting waves of change brought by overuse, urban sprawl, invasive species, pollution and global climate change.

legacy left to us by Lewis and Clark. "They were the first to imprint the significant landscape of the West and Northwest on our nation's imagination," he says. Thomas Jefferson, who conceived the expedition, equally understood the magnitude of the achievement. "We shall delineate with correctness the great arteries of this country," he declared. "Those who come after us will fill up the canvas we begin."

Trail of Tears National Historic Trail

From Conflict to Reconciliation

SMART MOUNTAIN, Tennessee, is cloaked in conifers that shade the twin grooves of a sheer mountain road. "Those ruts made me cry when I first saw them, they cut so deeply into the ground," says Trail of Tears Association board member Mary Tidwell. "Suddenly I felt my Cherokee ancestors walking through those woods. I saw them jam logs between wheel spokes to keep their wagons from plummeting headlong into the river below. I looked for the caves where my people huddled against the November rain. I looked for the shallow indentations in the ground where their graves may be."

The Trail of Tears is unlike most other pathways in the National Trails System. It is a reminder of injustice, a memorial to the Americans who died

> Children cry and many men cry... but they say nothing and just put heads down and keep on go towards West. Many days pass and people die very much.
>
> *Recollections of a survivor*

along it and to those who lived to remember. It tells a story of broken treaties, land theft and displacement of Native peoples by white settlers. It relates the story of a proud and dignified exodus westward.

The Cherokee removal, ordered by President Andrew Jackson and sanctioned by Congress, was resisted vigorously by the Cherokee through legal actions. The removal was finally carried out by President Martin Van Buren in 1838, despite a Supreme Court decision barring it.

Roughly 16,000 Cherokee were marched from their forest homeland in the Appalachians to the treeless plains of Indian Territory, now the state of Oklahoma. First-person accounts offer parallels to 20th century ethnic cleansing. "I saw the helpless Cherokees arrested and dragged from their homes and driven at the bayonet point into the stockades," wrote U.S. Army Private John G. Burnett. "And in the chill of a drizzling rain on an October morning I saw them loaded like cattle or sheep into six hundred and forty-five wagons and headed for the West."

Harsh winter weather, treacherous river crossings, exhaustion, malnutrition and smallpox claimed many. The initial roundup and detention and then the march and its aftermath may have killed up to 4,000 people. "In 1840, no one would have believed that the tribe could survive," says Paul Austin, executive secretary of the Trail of Tears Association. "But they did survive and thrive as a resilient Native American Nation." Today, vibrant Cherokee communities exist in both North Carolina and Oklahoma.

In 1987, the U.S. Congress designated the Trail of Tears as a national historic trail, commemorating the sorrowful journey west. Today, the Trail is administered by the National Park Service in a strong partnership with the Cherokee Nation, the Eastern Band of Cherokee Indians, the Trail of Tears Association, other federal agencies (such as the Tennessee Valley Authority, U.S. Forest Service, U.S. Army and Corps of Engineers), state and local organizations and private landowners. It is the NPS role to stimulate stewardship of resources by others and to facilitate the development of wayside exhibits, museum and traveling exhibits, site bulletins, brochures, mapping projects, historical and archeological research projects and newsletters that help the public understand the Trail of Tears.

Exhibits and dioramas interpret the Trail's story at the newly remodeled Museum of the Cherokee Indian in Cherokee, N.C. COURTESY MUSEUM OF THE CHEROKEE NATION

Remnants of the Trail of Tears in eastern Tennessee are proposed for a conservation easement. ©NATIONAL PARK SERVICE

this was my first trip East. I nodded 'yes.' She smiled up at me and said, 'so you finally decided to come home?' Suddenly I recognized what we had all lost."

The NPS and volunteers—both American Indian and non-American Indian—have perpetuated the Trail of Tears story. They are making sure that the routes originally used in the exodus—the federally designated northern land route and southern water route, plus the unofficial Benge's and Bell's routes—are being researched. Nine states have established Trail of Tears Association chapters.

At the Trail's starting points in Tennessee, North Carolina, Georgia and Alabama, the holding forts—internment camps where the Cherokee were herded together and held before the march west—are being studied by archeologists. Tennessee volunteers have sought to protect private property over which the Trail runs.

At Trail's end, the graves of those who arrived alive in Indian Territory have been marked with plaques. Major museums—the Cherokee Heritage Museum in Tahlequah, Oklahoma, and the Museum of the Cherokee in Cherokee, North Carolina—have long been well established. Educational videos and in-depth school curricula are planned. "People are hungry for knowledge about the Trail," says Mary Tidwell, a member of the Trail of Tears

"The event itself is the Trail," asserts Paul Austin, listing the many modern journeys made in remembrance of the removal. Cherokee teens, for example, recently biked the marked auto tour route from Oklahoma to North Carolina. The NPS is working with volunteers to establish hiking trails along portions of the historic route.

Government and nonprofit groups have also organized historical conferences to keep the memory alive. "The first time I came to North Carolina for a Trail of Tears symposium," relates

We will never let our hold to this land go . . . to let it go it will be like throwing away . . . (our) mother that gave . . . (us) birth.

Aitooweyah

Mary Tidwell, an Oklahoma Cherokee, "we had lunch at a retirement home. An Eastern Cherokee elder asked me if

James Vann, a wealthy Cherokee chief, had this house built in 1805. It is now a certified site of the Trail of Tears.

National Historic Trail Advisory Council, "but we need much more federal support. There's just not enough of me to go around!"

Today, the Trail of Tears is not only a memorial to one tribe's suffering. It provides an opportunity to relate the story of the other American Indian removals perpetuated by the U.S. government. At Fort Smith National Historical Park in Arkansas, for example, volunteers retell the tragic removals of the Cherokee, Chickasaw, Choctaw, Creek and Seminole tribes.

"My great-great grandmother died and was buried somewhere on the Trail of Tears. I have no idea where," Mary Tidwell says. "I couldn't do anything for her to stop that terrible thing from happening. But all of America can act now and try to end the alienation, alcoholism, illiteracy and other ills attributed to a loss of culture. You have to know the past to go forward."

Santa Fe National Historic Trail

Preserving the Great Prairie Highway

WALTER SHARP WAS A Kansas farmer, octogenarian, chain smoker and proud owner of a small chunk of the Santa Fe Trail. "He spent a magic hour showing me the wagon ruts on his property," remembers Santa Fe Trail Association President Margaret Sears. "As we walked the swales, he told me about his life: about his move from Kansas City back to the farm, of losing his wife earlier that year and about his boys. Then he pointed to a buffalo wallow. He was so gleeful to show me something I'd never seen before.

"It's people like Mr. Sharp who kept the Santa Fe Trail alive, long before we in the Trail Association and the National Park Service came along," Sears confides. "Those private land holders had nothing to gain by it. They've given so much back to our community, and they did it only out of love."

But Sears is too modest—were it not for the efforts of the Santa Fe Trail Association and the National Park Service, many miles of wagon ruts, plus numerous historic landmarks, might have long since disappeared beneath plow and pavement.

The 900-plus-mile Santa Fe Trail is one of the world's legendary trade routes, evoking romantic frontier images of hearty freight wagoneers and campfires under prairie stars. Long after the Trail was abandoned, it stayed etched on the landscape and in the American imagination.

The Santa Fe Trail was born with Mexico's successful revolt against Spain (opening the door to trade with the United States), and through the entre-preneurial spirit of a farmer down on his luck.

"As of 1821, William Becknell was bankrupt," relates historian Marc Simmons. "All of a sudden he got a bright idea to become a traveling merchant, to . . . put together a mule train loaded with trade goods, strike out across the Kansas Prairie, ascend the Arkansas River and cross the mountains to Santa Fe. There he sold his goods at enormous profit. With one bold stroke Becknell had opened a new international trail of commerce, turned his personal fortunes around and walked right into the history books."

The Santa Fe Trail tempted American and Mexican merchants with its promise of profit and tempered their judgment with its risks. A typical trip in 1824 parlayed $35,000 in American calicos and other wares into $190,000 in Mexican gold, silver and furs. But danger was never distant. The dust, heat and tedium of the eight-week journey could be shattered by fierce dust storms, wildfire or killing thirst.

For 50 years, wagon trains cut ever-deeper ruts into the Great Plains, as a river of commerce flowed both east and west past forts, small settlements and ranchos, across open prairie and Indian lands. The Santa Fe Trail com-mingled Anglo, Hispanic, Cheyenne, Arapaho, Kiowa, Comanche, Osage, Kansas (Kaw), Ute, Jicarilla Apache and other American Indian cultures.

The U.S. Army traveled the Trail in its 1846 invasion of Mexico, which secured New Mexico and Upper California for the U.S. After the Mexican American War, mail and stage

I can see the tired drivers at noonday lying under the shade of the wagons, their hats covering their faces . . . I can see the tired sweaty mules rolling over and over in the grass delighted to be free from the heavy wagons.

Marian Russell, remembering at age 89

coaches and military freight wagon trains composed the bulk of users.

While Indian attacks were a rare event on the real Santa Fe Trail, lurid circle-the-wagon tales inspired endless Hollywood cliches, like those seen in the 1940 film *Santa Fe Trail* starring Ronald Reagan. Forty-seven years later, the movie's star—now President of the

Santa Fe Trail marker in the Cimarron National Grasslands, southwest Kansas.

A Trail of Words: The Role of Journals, Newsletters and Websites

In 1939, two years after the "completion" of the Appalachian Trail, Maine native Jean Stephenson launched a tiny journal to document the unfolding fortunes of America's first long distance trail.

Today, the *Appalachian Trailway News* is joined by numerous association newsletters: by the Lewis and Clark Trail Heritage Foundation's *We Proceeded On,* by the Continental Divide Trail News, Pony Express *Trail Gazette,* the Florida Trail Association's *Footprint* and the Santa Fe Trail Association's *Wagon Tracks,* to name a few.

These journals, often edited by volunteers, are written by trail users and maintainers, staffers and government partners, professional ethnographers, amateur historians, beginning biologists and Ph.D. botanists.

Do you want to know what Juan Bautista de Anza's cavalryman uniforms looked like? (Hint: the soldiers didn't wear Conquistador armor!)

Do you want to know what prairie animal courtship behaviors Lewis and Clark witnessed? (Spring displays by excited dancing male sharptail grouse and the rutting of wapiti and bison.)

Care to find out what John Brinda ate on his 6,000-mile hike from Key West, Florida, along the Appalachian Trail, to Canada's International Appalachian Trail? (His adventure was fueled exclusively by Grape Nuts and French fries.)

Today, American Hiking Society, a national recreation-based conservation organization, publishes *Pathways Across America,* a newsletter financed by the National Park service and edited by the Partnership for the National Trails System, to inspire anyone involved with national scenic and historic trails.

National trail nonprofit newsletters are sometimes profound, sometimes esoteric, quirky or funny but almost always fascinating. There's probably no quicker way to get immersed in a trail's history and culture, unless you log-on to its website.

United States—signed a bill designating the Santa Fe Trail as a National Historic Trail. John Cook, Southwest regional director for the National Park Service at the time, declared the Santa Fe Trail to be as valuable to the American people as the Grand Canyon or Yellowstone.

Today, the Trail's historic and auto-tour routes pass through five states, connect with hundreds of historic sites and offer up many miles of authentic wagon ruts. The National Frontier Trails Center in Independence, Missouri, near the eastern end of the Trail; Fort Larned and the recreated

Bent's Old Fort National Historic Sites; inscriptions at Autograph Rock in Oklahoma; plus the skeletal ruins of Fort Union in New Mexico are just a few favorite stopping points. Trail markers placed by the Daughters of the American Revolution in the early 1900s still enlighten tourists. Hikers and equestrians enjoy the 20 miles of companion trail along the historic route provided by the USDA Forest Service across the Cimarron National Grassland.

Visitors enjoy an interpretive exhibit at the Neosho River crossing of the Santa Fe Trail in Council Grove, Kansas.

The National Park Service, in cooperation with the SFTA, state and local organizations, works hard to map the Trail, preserve and certify historic sites, advocate for conservation easements and land donations, develop wayside and museum exhibits and generate

NPS provided funding for a rock inscription project at Autograph Rock, a certified Trail site in western Oklahoma.

publications, including an award-winning map and guide. Private property holders play a key part. Oklahoma ranchers Dan and Carol Sharp—who protected Autograph Rock for many years—were the first to sign a voluntary certification agreement with the NPS for a Santa Fe Trail historic site. They joined with NPS and volunteers to develop the site for visitors while protecting its resources, and now support efforts to research and preserve Autograph Rock inscriptions.

"The Trail today is still a great adventure," says Margaret Sears. "It's the people you meet along the way, that's where you'll find the passion, marvelous people searching out history and making the same journey you are."

Oregon National Historic Trail

Tales of the Great Western Migration

NEAR GUERNSEY, Wyoming, today's visitors see the impact of 400,000 emigrants who left the United States to seek a new life in far-off Oregon. At Deep Rut Hill, amid growths of pinion pine, the passage of countless iron-rimmed wagon wheels has carved ruts five feet deep in the limestone.

"When people climb this hill today and look, their mouths drop open," says historian Gregory Franzwa. "They usually exclaim, 'Oh my God!' with sudden understanding."

Two other landmarks nearby, Register Cliff and a small concrete obelisk, document less dramatic but poignant impacts upon the land. On Register Cliff, hopeful emigrants inscribed their names in stone. Beneath the concrete marker rests Lucindy Rollins, one of 30,000 wagoneers who never saw Oregon.

Beginning in 1841, the Oregon Trail beckoned to Americans who wanted to better their lot: to New England farmers whose fields yielded more rocks than potatoes and to Midwesterners beset by economic downturns (then called "panics"). Mythical Oregon called to all with its pigs "running about under the great acorn trees, round and fat, and already cooked, with knives and forks sticking in them so that you can cut off a slice whenever you are hungry."

Farm wagons were changed into prairie schooners on the road West. Oregon Trail caravans flowed for 40 years from Independence, Missouri, overland to the Platte River at Fort Kearny (gateway to the Great Plains), across the Continental Divide at South Pass and on to Fort Bridger, where those bound for Oregon, California and Utah sorted themselves out.

Those bound for the Northwest raced on against winter snows across the rugged Snake River Plateau and the Blue Mountains. In the early days, the travelers made a swift but treacherous journey down the Columbia River by raft or, after 1846, trekked over the high Cascades by wagon on the Barlow Road, "exposed like a bug on a table." Finally, they rolled down into the Promised Land of Oregon's Willamette Valley.

"Remember, this wasn't the U.S. Army moving out to claim new territory but plain ordinary human beings—

mom, dad, the kids and grandma—giving us a valid claim to the Northwest," reminds Gregory Franzwa, founding president of the Oregon-California Trails Association (OCTA). "It was they who first established our nation's coast-to-coast reality."

The Oregon Trail exists today not only in its many miles of wagon ruts and historic sites, but also in the collective memory of the emigrants. OCTA has collected more than 900 diaries recording the everyday tedium, wonder and horror of life on the move: "Dust is frequently more than shoe deep, and if the wind happens to blow you cannot see the next wagon in

Eastward I go only by force, but westward I go free. This is the prevailing tendency of my countrymen. I must walk toward Oregon.

Henry David Thoreau

front," writes James Field in 1845. "We could not walk for dung and could not breathe for the smell of dead oxen," says Agnes Stewart Warner.

"A restless night; the dogs bark, the wolves prowl, the horses take fright and break loose; the Indians about are watching for an opportunity to take whatever they can get—all cause our sleep to be filled with anxiety and

Wagon train near upper Sweetwater River, Wyoming. ©NATIONAL PARK SERVICE

Guernsey Ruts State Park, Wyoming © LINDA RAY—NATIONAL PARK SERVICE

dreams," bemoans Narcissa Whitman.

"Our camp this evening presents a most cheerful appearance. The numerous white tents and wagon-covers

Why did such men peril everything, exposing their helpless families to the possibilities of massacre and starvation, braving death—and for what purpose? I am not quite certain that any rational answer will ever be given to that question.

James Nesmith, 1843

before which the campfires are blazing brightly represent a rustic village; and men, women and children are talking, playing, and singing around them," comments a joyful emigrant writer.

"There have been many deaths. 'Tis a hard thing to die far from friends and home—to be buried in a hastily dug grave—without shroud or coffin—the clods filled in and then deserted, perhaps to be food for wolves," laments Esther Hanna.

Finally, Oregon! "Here husband traded two yoke of oxen for a half section of land with one-half acre planted in potatoes and a small cabin. This is the journey's end," writes Amelia Knight with gentle understatement.

"Each journal is remarkable," says Gregory Franzwa, "These are people who walked 15 to 20 miles each day through heat and dust, yet spent time each evening writing in their diaries. They knew something very incredible was happening in their lives and the life of the country."

Designated a National Historic Trail in 1978, the Oregon Trail today inspires new adventures. The volunteers of OCTA, along with their National Park Service partner, seek to map and mark the original Trail.

Don Popejoy recalls his 1998 volunteer stint on a trail-marking trip to Pelican Creek, Oregon. He bumped over mountain roads in a 4 x 4, struggled afoot up escarpments and through pine forests, tried to comprehend a TV-remote-control-sized satellite global positioning unit used to ascertain the Oregon Trail's main route and then pounded six-foot-long Carsonite trail markers into hard ground for days on end.

"We're on our way!" declares OCTA past President Dr. Roger Blair. "We've converted the Bureau of Land Management and U.S. Forest Service into two of our best partners. Where once they might have obliterated ruts with logging roads and pipelines, they now carefully protect Trail traces. Education and awareness remain our best opportunity to protect the Oregon Trail, and all historic trails, for the future."

Mormon Pioneer National Historic Trail

Pilgrimage to Zion

ATOP ANCIENT RUINS BLUFF, Nebraska, you can look farther and see less than almost anywhere else along the Mormon Trail. An enormous sweep of open prairie—the vast level floodplain of the Platte River—stretches out in all directions.

"What you see is the hand of God, not the works of man," says Mormon Trails Association historian Stanley Kimball. But not quite: "If I tell you just where to look, you'll spy a hundred yards of ruts," the faintly visible path by which 70,000 Mormons moved beyond the borders of the United States to Utah between 1846 and 1869. "It's like looking through a window into history."

Hurra, hurra, hurra, there's my home at last!

Thomas Bullock, July 22, 1847, on first seeing the Great Salt Lake Valley

The great Mormon emigration is a vital chapter in the history of the American West. Yet it stands apart, for the Mormons, unlike families seeking homes in Oregon or adventurers searching for California gold, had a different vision. "They were driven 'from civilization to sundown' for religious freedom," writes Stanley Kimball. "They moved as villages on wheels—a whole culture, a faith, a people going west." Their journey through the wilderness, born out of persecution, is often compared to the Bible's Exodus. Prophet Brigham Young (sometimes called the "Mormon Moses") was the charismatic leader who led these modern "Children of Israel to the Promised Land."

The Church of Jesus Christ of Latter-day Saints was founded by Joseph Smith in 1830, when, according to Mormon history, he received inscribed golden plates from an angel. These plates, the Book of Mormon, proclaimed the restoration of the true church of Jesus Christ in modern times, to be led by contemporary prophets who spoke directly with God.

Mormon beliefs, which stood outside mainstream Christian tradition, helped fuel intolerance. Persecution forced the rapidly expanding Church west, from New York to Ohio, then to Missouri (where the state passed a

Mormon Pioneer wagon train reenactment, 1997

© LDS HISTORICAL DEPT. ARCHIVES

Mormon "Extermination Act"), and then onto swampland in Illinois. Here the Mormons built Nauvoo, a model city of 11,000 (then the tenth largest U.S. town).

Violence erupted in 1844, when an angry mob murdered founding prophet Joseph Smith. Church members elected Brigham Young as their new leader and decided to move their brethren yet again, this time out of the country. During the savage rains of

February, 1846, 4,000 Mormons abandoned their homes and launched the best organized mass migration in American history.

In the first year they covered just 265 miles, crossing Iowa and arriving at Winter Quarters (now Omaha, Nebraska) on the Missouri River. After a hard winter, an advance party of 145 headed west along the Platte River on the opposite side from the Oregon

The Mormon Trail ran both ways. Trains of "down and back" missionaries headed back east to bring more brethren to Zion.

Trail. At Fort Bridger, they used explorer John Fremont's journal to guide them into the Wasatch Mountains, over red rock ridges and through willow-choked canyons.

In July 1847, they completed their 1,300-mile trek, arriving at Utah's Great Basin and Great Salt Lake. Here they founded the independent state of Deseret (never mind that they were officially on Mexican soil!). They laid out streets in the barren desert, built shelters, dug irrigation ditches, planted potatoes, corn, beans, turnips and buckwheat.

Brigham Young almost immediately headed east to bring more of his brethren into Zion. "That's one of the big differences between the Mormon Trail and other western trails," says

Mormon Trails Association President Gar Elison. "It ran in both directions. In fact, the Mormons helped create the infrastructure for western expansion. They improved the Trail, built bridges, established ferries, measured mileage (with an odometer of their own making), scientifically mapped the path, and established way stations, where crops were planted to feed future emigrants."

A Perpetual Emigration Fund was established to help newly converted Mormons come west. The emigrants always traveled in disciplined companies of 100s, 50s, and 10s, so they were able to offer mutual assistance. No wonder the beehive remains an important symbol of the Mormon Church. Despite these feats of organization, this was no easy trip, and for many it was the ultimate test of faith. Six thousand died in the crossing. Then, in 1869, the railroad came to Promontory Point, close enough to Salt Lake City that the Trail fell into disuse.

In 1978, the Mormon Pioneer Trail was designated a National Historic Trail. Today, 822 miles are in private hands, with 264 miles on federal lands, and 214 in state management. The Trail's diverse partnership includes several state-wide nonprofit Mormon trails associations, the National Park Service as Trail administrator, the USDA Forest Service, Bureau of Land Management, Church of Jesus Christ of Latter-day Saints, private landowners, historical societies, plus state tourism and economic development departments. "To me, and to many Mormons, the Trail is a linear temple, one of the most sacred of religious experiences," says Stanley Kimball.

Come, come ye Saints, No toil nor labor fear, But with joy wend your way. We'll find a place which God for us prepared, Far away in the West.

William Clayton, April 1846

The Mormon Trails Association and National Park Service today face the same challenges as stewards of other National Historic Trails. They race to identify and mark historic sites and alternate routes before they are obliterated by development, and to interpret and publicize the Trail via waysides, museums, guidebooks and a website for a general public hungry for history. "There seems to be a direct relationship between the speed with which we destroy our national heritage," Kimball states with irony, "and our desire to go in search of it, to experience the power of place and the spirit of locale."

California National Historic Trail

Gold Rush!

JOHN CLARK AND 250,000 California Trail travelers experienced the stark beauty of the Great American Desert firsthand: "Great God, I thought, what a sight lay before us," he writes in 1852. "Long ridges, dry knobs, deep gullies, few flowers, and short grass; now & then a stunted grove of lonely oak and for miles hundreds of teams stretching forward like a great Caravan in line on the dark & winding trace leading toward the setting sun."

> Boys, by God, I believe I have found a gold mine!
>
> *James Marshall, on discovering gold at Sutter's Fort, 1848*

Gold! The cry went out from Sutter's Mill, California, in 1848. Within a year, a stampede of 25,000 greenhorn gold seekers poured out of the East and overland along the California Trail—doubling in 12 months the number of emigrants that had passed to Oregon and California between 1841 and 1848.

Viewed on a map, the California Trail winds west like a great rope, wild-ly frayed by its eastern feeders, central cutoffs and myriad western routes. At the Midwestern River towns of Independence, Westport, St. Joseph, Nebraska City and Council Bluffs, wagon outfitters did a brisk business. Farther west, the Trail routes merged, following the Platte River. But even this path was not one: trails ran on both sides of the stream, and, where easy prairie terrain allowed, the caravans spread out many wagons wide and one wagon long to avoid eating each other's dust.

Reaching the Rocky Mountains, the rope frayed still further into the Sublette, Salt Lake, and Hastings Cutoffs (the route used by the ill-fated Donner-Reed party, who were trapped by blizzards, forced into starvation and cannibalism). Most routes converged on Nevada's Humboldt River but diverged again in the Sierra Nevada Mountains to cross seven different passes, before flowing into the California gold fields.

When Congress designated the California Trail as a National Historic Trail in 1992, it selected many of its alternate routes and cutoffs for protection, establishing a daunting mission for land managers.

"What's so challenging about the California Trail is how much there is of it, over 5,600 miles," says Kay Threlkeld, interpretive planner for the National Park Service Long Distance Trails Office in Salt Lake City. "With just three people, our office oversees the California, Oregon, Mormon Pioneer and Pony Express Trails—that's 13,000 miles in total! Obviously, we don't have the people-power. But national trails aren't exactly like national parks; we depend on a cadre of local volunteers from the nonprofit trail associations to do the real work on the ground."

That cooperative workload is massive. It includes the mapping and marking of historic and auto routes, certifying of historic sites (more than 250 locations on the California Trail are proposed for protection), archeological digs, the building of waysides and interpretive centers, the publica-

"Independence Rock," a painting by William Henry Jackson, from the Jackson Collection at Scotts Bluff National Monument in western Nebraska. ©NATIONAL PARK SERVICE

Independence Rock, Wyoming. It was the goal of every wagon train to reach this famous landmark by July 4th.

tion of scholarly research, brochures and books, plus the creation of a vast database and website, a sort of "virtual California Trail" with maps, photos and diary entries.

> There we were, about to take off on a wagon train at a mule's pace; me with a laptop, a printer run off of a cigarette lighter, but no satellite up-link!
>
> *Kay Threlkeld, 1999 wagon train*

One innovative project relies on new technology to find old routes. "I've been looking at the physical impacts of trails on the environment, examining how they alter plant communities and soils," explains April Whitten, a University of Nebraska graduate student and Trail volunteer. "Then I use satellite imaging to see if those changes on the ground are identifiable spectrally from space." Her research is identifying precise pioneer routes—many used by Americans Indians for generations before the wagons came. "Our travels and migrations are one of the hallmarks of our humanity," says Whitten. "We're always looking for new homes, new ways to make a living, and we never take the straightest course but zigzag along the path of least resistance."

In 1999, California Trail partners celebrated the 150th anniversary of the Gold Rush by again sending wagons westward. The five-month journey (similar reenactments have been held along the Mormon Pioneer and Oregon Trails) attracted history buffs, seniors and families eager to rough it. "We want to do this to be with our horses," Ron Prettyman told the

Emigrant names carved in the rock's granite surface.

Elko, Nevada, *Daily Free Press*. "We don't want alarm clocks. We don't want people telling us what to do. Nine-to-five just don't cut it."

Kay Threlkeld, in period dress and performing living history demonstrations, walked or rode beside her National Park Service wagon. "It's not too bad. There's no beans or hard tack. A caterer feeds you dinner, and we use port-a-potties at night. After all, there are certain things you could do on the open prairie in 1849 that you can't do in 1999."

"It's a thrill," adds Dr. Roger Blair, former president of the Oregon-California Trails Association. "You gain a real appreciation for the pioneers. It's hot, dusty, you get bounced hard, and come off the wagon everyday with sunburn. The experience gave me as much insight into the hardships as I ever want to have."

Most of those who first traveled the California Trail never discovered a fortune in gold, though many did find futures in the West. By the late 1870s the railroad erased the need for overland wagon adventures. "The California Trail represents a very brief moment in our history, but it opened our nation," says April Whitten. "That's why we must save the Trail for posterity."

Pony Express National Historic Trail

The World's Most Renowned Mail Route

"IT'S A THRILL to stand in the western desert, see the sun go down, the stars brighten and wait for the mail to come," Patrick Hearty says as he recalls a 1998 Pony Express re-ride. "You strain your eyes against the blackness. Then a horse pounds out of the dark. The rider dismounts, and hands over the mochilla, the leather mail pouch. You throw it over your saddle tree, leap up and gallop away. Alone now, you feel the power of the animal beneath you and sense the ghosts of Pony Express riders swirling around you."

In its brief, meteoric life the Pony Express service covered 600,000 miles, delivered more than 34,000 pieces of mail and made a lasting impact on history and myth.

Visionary businessman William Russell, with partners A. Majors and W.B. Waddel, launched the risky ven-

> A man and horse burst past our excited faces, and go winging away like a belated fragment of a storm!
>
> *Mark Twain,* Roughing It

ture. Between April 1860 and October 1861, the red-shirted Pony Express riders braved Indian arrows, searing heat and raging storm to bring urgent news of Lincoln's inauguration and word of the Rebel firing on Fort Sumter to the new state of California.

Messages that would have languished six weeks aboard ship reached San Francisco overland in under ten days. The speed of the Pony Express helped keep California in the Union and made a legend of its riders.

They were tough young men, built like jockeys, weighing in at 120 pounds or less. They rode the best horse-flesh money could buy, usually wild California mustangs. Rider Nick Wilson maintained that Pony Express horses were considered broken "when a hostler could lead them into and out of the stable without getting his head kicked off," but, he added, "very likely they had been handled just enough to make them mean."

Horse and rider traveled light, carrying the mochilla, 20 pounds of mail, rifle and Colt revolver. Riders typically covered 50 miles before passing the mail to the next rider, going from home station to home station, and changing horses at way stations set ten miles apart. The service, so famous for its lightning speed, became obsolete when the telegraph cut transcontinental communication time to four hours.

Modern Pony Express National Historic Trail re-riders are a somewhat different breed from their historic counterparts. When a National Pony Express Association (NPEA) officer looked out over the newest crop of middle-aged history buffs and equestrians to whom he was about to administer the Pony Express Oath, he joked by quoting the service's 1860 purported employment ad: "Not too many of you appear to be 'young, skinny, wiry fellows, or orphans,'" he said, "but I do believe you will be 'willing to risk death daily!'"

Today's NPEA members recreate Pony Express mail service every June, when more than 500 re-riders speed commemorative mail along the 1,900-mile route from St. Joseph, Missouri, up the Platte River on the California and Oregon Trails, through South Pass and the Rockies to Salt Lake City, across the Utah-Nevada desert, over the Sierras and on to San Francisco.

Devil's Gate, Wyoming ©NATIONAL PARK SERVICE

Trail ruts (left side), Rock Creek Station State Historical Park, Nebraska—once a station on the Pony Express.

"We carry the commemorative letters as a fund raiser," explains former NPEA President Patrick Hearty. "Anyone can send a letter for $5, the same price as in 1860."

In 1983, NPEA re-riders aided the U.S. Postal Service by delivering 1,800 pieces of mail per week to California towns cut off by a mudslide in the American River Canyon. In 1996, re-riders carried the Olympic Torch for 500 miles as it traveled to the Summer Games in Atlanta. Still other re-riders braved prairie thunder storms to deliver mail to the Mormon Pioneer Trail Commemorative Wagon Train in 1997. When not doing re-rides, the NPEA and National Park Service work to mark, preserve and promote the Trail.

Joe Nardone, executive director of the Pony Express Trail Association, hopes to make the Pony Express Trail experience available to all Americans. "I've hiked the Trail (in five months), ridden it on horseback (three months), mountain biked it (57 days), driven as much of it as I legally could in a 4x4 (ten days) and flown it (twelve hours). This year I'm doing it by motorcycle, and the year after next, by RV. Friends want to know whether I'll go by pogo stick. No, I tell them, but I am considering electric car." Nardone's trips will serve as research for a comprehensive guidebook that delineates which uses are appropriate on which Trail segments.

NPEA and NPS have other ambitious goals for the Trail, designated a National Historic Trail in 1992. "In the next ten years we want to see all of

Reenactors, Re-riders, Rut Nuts and Thru-Hikers

(Or, how national trails changed my life forever)

A New York-New Jersey Trail Conference writer documenting the first rush to America's trails in the 1930s described his fellows as "no fair-weather strollers . . . knights of brush and brier . . . without fear and above reproach. It would be superfluous to add that they are enthusiasts, and perhaps they are slightly tinged with madness."

Trail madness has seized many Americans since those days.

Thru-hikers on the Pacific Crest Trail endure months of desert heat, terrible cold, wet feet and soggy oatmeal to walk the 2,638-mile path. At journey's end they are rewarded with a colorful arm patch.

Rut nuts on the California Trail endure bone-jarring journeys across rugged mountain terrain via four-wheeler to view a mere hundred feet of grooved ground—the ghostly imprint of westward-bound wagons.

Reenactors and re-riders are other enthusiasts. Modern wagon trains roll west on the Oregon Trail, while contemporary Pony Express re-riders hurl themselves headlong into the desert night. On the Overmountain Victory Trail, squads of buck-skinned reenactors annually demonstrate their flint-lock rifles.

What is the value in these experiences? Those interviewed for this book agree: national trails can make ordinary people's lives extraordinary. For some "mad" reason, trails evoke passion from us. They are a call to adventure. That is their draw, their magic.

the historical trail marked and interpreted for the education and enjoyment of the public," says Patrick Hearty.

NPEA members, like other National Trail enthusiasts, have a deep fascination for their Trail and its story, but they possess an added dimension: their passion for horses. "My granddad was a Utah homesteader and cattle rancher. I'm a chemist," explains Hearty. "Still, horses hold a fascination for me, with their beauty, power and majesty. I love to let that power loose, to throw a mochilla over the saddle and ride off to deliver the mail."

Scenery, solitude, stillness: the physical trail is as varied as America.

Patrick Hearty, former president, National Pony Express Association

Nez Perce (Nee-Me-Poo) National Historic Trail

A Path of Sadness, Courage and Remembrance

DEEP IN THE BITTERROOT Mountains near Lolo Pass, a high subalpine meadow blooms each June with camas, a blue lily. The surrounding forest of tall firs, huckleberry and heather is little changed since the Nez Perce people first blazed an ancient trail here thousands of years ago.

Nor has it changed much since 1877, that infamous year when five Nez Perce bands fled their homeland and crossed this pass in a heroic, but futile, effort to escape the U.S. Army. "The land up there is sacred ground to us," says Otis Halfmoon, former manager of the Nez Perce National Historic Park. "This was our Trail to Buffalo Country, for trade and communica-

> Our chiefs are killed. It is cold and we have no blankets. The little children are freezing to death; I am tired; my heart is sick and sad. From where the sun now stands, I will fight no more forever.
>
> *Chief Joseph, surrender at Bear's Paw Mountains, October 5, 1877*

tion. It holds vision quest sites and burials."

The sky glowed deeply blue over this same green meadow in the summer of 1991, when diverse groups that had once faced each other in war gathered together in peace to dedicate the Nez Perce National Historic Trail.

"This Trail is different from most other National Trails," says Keith Thurkill, USDA Forest Service coordinator for the Nez Perce National Historic Trail. "It shouldn't be viewed as a recreational park but as a serious place, to be respected. The story told by the Trail is of a tragic war that broke out, despite the many leaders who tried to prevent it. What happened here needs to be understood as what also happened to other American Indian tribes, and what continues to happen the world over when indigenous peoples are encroached upon by powerful immigrants. It's a story as current as today's headlines."

The Nez Perce (who call themselves the Nee-Me-Poo, "the People") once claimed the vast plateau country of ancient volcanic rock, deep canyons and wild rivers stretching between the Cascades and Rocky Mountains as their homeland. "This was our country for generation upon generation," says Otis Halfmoon, "so long ago that there are stories of hunting mammoth."

In 1805, the Nez Perce aided Lewis and Clark. They welcomed fur traders and missionaries to their beautiful and abundant land. In 1855, a growing settler population forced the Nez Perce onto a 5,000-square-mile reservation.

The discovery of gold and an invasion by prospectors in 1860 resulted in the contested Treaty of 1863, reducing Nez Perce lands ten-fold. This treaty, signed by just a few Nez Perce bands, lacked tribal authority. The remaining bands, whose lands weren't included in the reservation at Lapwai, Idaho, refused to sign and became known as the "nontreaty" Nez Perce.

The U.S. Army ordered the five nontreaty bands onto the reservation in 1877. Rather than risk war, they agreed. But pent-up anger, stemming from years of mistreatment by whites, moved several young warriors to kill white settlers. The hope for a peaceful move to the reservation vanished, and 750 Nez Perce became fugitives in

Camas Lily prairie near Lapwai, ID. ©USDA FOREST SERVICE

Protecting Sacred Sites

"The Nez Perce Trail is viewed by the Nee-Me-Poo bands and the National Park Service as a linear graveyard," says Keith Thurkill, USDA Forest Service Coordinator for the NPNHT. Similarly, the Trail of Tears (where as many as 4,000 Cherokee died) and the Oregon Trail (lined by 40,000 pioneer graves) are perceived as sacred ground.

Burials aren't the only sacred sites found along national trail corridors. The Nez Perce Trail, for example, saw centuries of American Indian use. Nee-Me-Poo medicine rings and prayer ceremony sites line the path like jewels on a strand.

But identifying sacred sites isn't always easy. Mysterious rock cairns dot the Nez Perce Trail: They may be explained as markers left by herdsmen or miners, sites of sacred vision quests or as prayer monuments offered over centuries by individuals (called "Tam-loy yiic max," wherein "one left a memorial to oneself and found one's old self"). Trail stewards must struggle to decipher whether such perplexing artifacts warrant protection.

With growing national trail use, land managers face the challenging task of balancing the needs and values of diverse trail users—tribal peoples, traditionalists, historians, equestrians, bicyclists, hikers and sightseers—against the necessity to respect sacred sites.

their own ancestral homeland.

They fled Idaho and, for the next four months, fought and outwitted a succession of U.S. Army commanders. The Nez Perce followed a circuitous 1,000-mile escape route, first heading east toward Crow allies on the Great Plains, then north toward Canada. Desperate defensive battles bloodied the path, as both Nez Perce and soldiers died. Finally, trapped and surrounded, they surrendered near Montana's Bear's Paw Mountains just 40 miles from the Canadian border. The captive Nez Perce were exiled to reservations far from their homeland.

The Nez Perce Trail was designated a national historic trail by Congress in 1986. Its 1,170-mile route follows the path of flight taken by the Nontreaty Nez Perce. It crosses a vast mosaic of federal, state, tribal and private lands. The Trail is administered by the USDA Forest Service. The National Park Service manages 38 sites along the Trail. The nonprofit Nez Perce National Historic Trail Foundation,

> What the Nez Perce Trail offers to all of us in the 21st century is an opportunity for reconciliation and understanding.
>
> *Otis Halfmoon, Manager,*
> *Nez Perce National Historic Park*

with strong tribal interests, provides advocacy and volunteer support.

An official auto-tour route has been designated and signed, and 79 historic places along or near the route are interpreted. Key sites include the White Bird Battlefield (where the outnumbered Nez Perce won an early victory), the Clearwater, Big Hole, Canyon Creek and Bear's Paw Battlefields, as well as the escape route through Yellowstone National Park in Wyoming.

The Trail is being developed with sensitivity, dignity and respect. "It is a memorial Trail, with a lot of dead people buried along it," says Charlie Moses, a member of the Joseph Band and vice-president of the Nez Perce National Historic Trail Foundation. "We don't want to see it overdeveloped, artifacts removed or graves touched. We're really not concerned that the actual Trail be clearly marked, but we are concerned that the story behind the Trail be told truthfully."

"My great-grandfather and great-great-grandmother were both killed on the Trail, at the Big Hole Battlefield,

©USDA FOREST SERVICE

on August 9, 1877. A hundred people were killed that day, babies' heads were smashed," Otis Halfmoon says softly. "What people can find today along the Nez Perce Trail is the truth about the so-called 'Indian Wars,' that it was a clash between two cultures and a fight for homeland at great cost, a concept that is very strong in every American's heart. What the Nez Perce Trail offers to all of us in the 21st century is an opportunity for reconciliation and understanding."

Iditarod National Historic Trail

The Last Great Race

HUNDREDS OF SLED DOGS yip, howl and strain in their traces, raising an unearthly din. Keyed up drivers hold the dogs back. Onlookers clap madly, though heavy mittens muffle their applause. Suddenly, a starter sends the teams flying along snowy Anchorage streets and into the Alaskan wilderness.

This is the Iditarod, "The Last Great Race," a grueling 11-day, 1,100-mile run that challenges human and beast. Mushers risk subzero temperatures, fierce spring storms and snowslides as they glide across three conifer-cloaked mountain ranges, barren tundra and frozen rivers with tongue-twisting names like Kuskokwim and Unalakleet—names that echo the land's Native heritage. The sleds pass ruined cabins, mines

Memories of the Frontier period in the rest of the country have faded into books and museums, but in Alaska some of the people who pushed to the edge of the frontier still live.

Tim Jones, Iditarod musher and author of
The Last Great Race

and roadhouses, reminders of the glory days of the Klondike gold rush. At last, the teams race into Nome on the Bering Sea, crossing the finish line to the sound of wailing sirens and in front of TV cameras.

"In New York, it's Yankee baseball, and in Indiana, basketball. In Alaska, it's mushing," says Mike Zaidlicz, Iditarod National Historic Trail administrator for the Bureau of Land Management. As many as 1,500 volunteers annually manage the Great Race. Dog handlers, checkers, cooks, bush pilots, ham radio operators, judges and veterinarians join in, as do the people who sew the hundreds of polar fleece booties worn by the dogs.

With the conclusion of the race each March, the Iditarod Trail drifts back into obscurity. "Of course, that's the biggest problem for us as an organization," says Leo Rasmussen, Nome mayor and president of Iditarod National Historic Trail, Incorporated (the Trail's nonprofit partner). "We need to get Alaskans to see the Iditarod as a National Trail, and not just as the Great Race. We need to build our Trail identity."

The Iditarod National Historic Trail, a 2,400-mile trail network with a 938-mile primary route, penetrates Alaska's wild interior and may be the granddaddy of all American pathways.

"It's probably the oldest trail in the western hemisphere. This is the path that first brought people onto the continent roughly 15,000 years ago," says Rasmussen. Paleolithic hunter-gatherers may have entered North America over the Beringia land bridge, connecting Alaska to Siberia during the last glacial age. "On the Iditarod Trail near Nome, archeologists have discovered pits marking the sites of sod igloos dating to 500 A.D. The Trail has been a trading route of the Ingalik and Tanaina Indians for centuries."

Then, in 1908, gold fever seized Alaska. At Seward in the south and Nome in the north, prospectors, known as "stampeders," hurriedly procured provisions before rushing inland along the Iditarod Trail to stake claims.

In 1910, the Army surveyed the Trail and named it the Seward to Nome Mail Trail. Sled dogs, a scruffy mix of mongrels and big-boned work dogs, hauled everything from pianos to mining equipment and fine bone china, though gold and news were the most treasured cargo.

In 1925, with planes about to replace sleds, mushers enjoyed a fleeting blaze of glory. A diphtheria epidemic threatened Nome, and a shortage of serum, plus bad weather (thwarting an airlift), prompted a daring rescue. A relay of 20 dog teams carried the serum 674 miles in 130 hours. Mushers were honored with Presidential medals, and sled dogs with statues. The Last Great Race, founded by Alaskan Joe Redington in 1967, commemorates the event.

"The Iditarod Trail is different from every other national trail; it exists only

Iditarod Race arrives in Nome.

How to Become a National Trail

There have been as many proposed national trails that have failed to receive congressional approval as there are designated national trails. The Koyukuk-Chandalar Trail in Alaska, Mormon Battalion Trail, Indian Nations Trail, and Jedediah Smith Trail, among others, have all failed to pass through the long, arduous process of congressional designation.

A proposed national trail must first gain the attention of Congress. Most are advocated by grassroots citizen organizations, though some, like the Natchez Trace Trail, are proposed by federal agencies.

Next, a congressional bill must authorize a feasibility study. Trail studies are conducted by a land-managing agency, usually the National Park Service. This lead agency takes on the tough task of bringing all of the players to the same table (or trail!). Federal, state and local governments, non-profit organizations and landowners all take part.

Trail proposals can be disqualified for many reasons: excessive costs, lack of public or government support, lack of national significance, land owner opposition, anticipated adverse impacts to ecosystems, or an inability to meet the feasibility criteria listed in the National Trails System Act. If the feasibility study is favorable, a bill establishing the trail must then be passed by Congress.

Finally, a comprehensive management plan is written. This document defines the trail and the management roles of its partners. Planning requirements are outlined in the National Trails System Act.

Congressional designation guarantees little. Volunteer and government partners must still work hard to transform the "paper trail" into an on-the-ground reality.

in winter, when tundra and rivers are frozen," says Mike Zaidlicz. "It's the only national trail on which you can see whales (near the southern terminus at Seward), seals, polar bear, caribou, wolves and walruses."

In winter, the Trail becomes a routinely traveled route between remote villages. School basketball teams jump on snow machines (what Alaskans call snowmobiles) and ride to the next town to compete with rivals. Every imaginable conveyance is raced on the Trail: sleds, skis, snow machines, mountain bikes, and more: "The first

300 yards of the Iditarod Trail in Nome go right down Main Street. That's where we hold our Great Bathtub Race," laughs Rasmussen.

The Trail today is administered by the Bureau of Land Management, in cooperation with other federal agencies, Native corporations, state and municipal agencies and private landowners. Most of its route crosses state of Alaska lands. Designated a National Historic Trail by Congress in 1978, the Iditarod Trail's volunteer effort is just now flourishing.

"We finally climbed out of the

bassinet with the formation of our nonprofit group in 1998," says Rasmussen. "We've begun marking Trail, selling log milepost tripods as a fundraiser. We're also assessing the Trail's 500 historical sites."

In a land as big as Alaska, management challenges loom. The Trail doesn't cross a road for 800 miles, and in terrain where caribou outnumber people, volunteer Trail maintainers are few. The elements also pose problems. Unwieldy log tripod trail markers are a must, because the carsonite posts used on historic trails in the Lower 48 would be swallowed up by boggy tundra.

"This is a Trail with a remarkable legacy," says Leo Rasmussen. "I've talked with people who sledded the Iditarod during the Gold Rush and to Native mail carriers. I met John Auliye, a 99-year-old Native American who carried the diphtheria serum in 1925 during the Race Against Death. Alaska is so close to its history that you can live here and feel a part of it."

The Iditarod Trail is a remnant of a not-too-distant past, not likely to be seen again.

Mike Zaidlicz, Administrator,
Iditarod National Historic Trail

Appalachian National Scenic Trail

Hike 2,150 Miles Along an Ancient Mountain Chain

AT AGE 41, BENTON MacKaye's life was a disaster. The obscure bureaucrat had been fired by Harvard University, forced out of his beloved Forest Service and shoved into a cubbyhole at the Labor Department. His visionary plans for social change had repeatedly fallen on deaf legislative ears. Then his wife, peace activist and suffragette Jessie Hardy Stubbs, committed suicide, drowning herself in New York's East River.

The grieving MacKaye sought solace in a childhood dream. As a boy, he had climbed a tall spruce atop Stratton Mountain, Vermont. From his perch he looked north and south along the billion-year-old spine of the Appalachian Mountain Range. He imagined a great hiking trail running from summit to summit. In 1921, just months after his wife's death, MacKaye

> To walk, to see, and to see what you see.
>
> *Benton MacKaye,*
> *when asked the purpose of*
> *the Appalachian Trail*

announced his bold idea to the world.

His proposal electrified northeastern hiking clubs. Within months their "elephant squads" took to the woods armed with pruning shears and paint brushes. By 1923, the first six miles of Appalachian Trail were open in New York's Harriman State Park. Within a few years, MacKaye moved on from the trail project. But others, fired up by the idea, replaced him. Maine lawyer Myron Avery saw the trail to completion in 1937.

Today, the Appalachian Trail follows ridgelines for 2,150 miles. Pegged down in the south by Springer Mountain, Georgia, it roams through lush magnolia and rhododendron forests, until eventually, it penetrates the vast silences of spruce and fir in the North Woods. After crossing 14 states, the Trail ends atop the granite sentinel of Mount Katahdin, Maine.

Along the way, its green corridor protects black bear and bobcat, rattlesnake and red eft (a tiny orange newt that often sits in the path, forcing hikers to step gingerly around).

The Trail is equally rich in human history. The path explores Native American rock shelters, Civil War battlefields, old homesteads and ruined iron mines. Place names along the Trail—Indian Grave Gap, Devils Tater Patch, Charlies Bunyan, Antietam Brook and Thoreau Falls—echo our heritage.

What made MacKaye's Appalachian Trail such a revolutionary idea was not the vastness of its conception, but the boundless source of its labor. MacKaye did not call upon government to build his trail, but upon volunteers. "Here is enormous undeveloped power—the spare time of our population," he wrote in his 1921 proposal. "Suppose just one percent of it were focused upon . . . increasing the facilities for the outdoor community life. This would be more than a million people."

MacKaye's volunteer army has stayed on the job for more than 75 years. No recruitment posters were ever needed to collect these forces. The mountains themselves did the job.

The rugged slate peaks in the Bigelow Mountain Range of Maine recruited Dave Field. "My brother was always leading me into escapades," Field recalls. "In 1955, he found a map with this trail stretched across it. We set off to explore. But Hurricane Carol had blasted through just two years earlier. We 'hiked,' 20 feet above the ground on fallen trees." The boys decided that someone ought to fix up this trail, and they spent the summer clearing blow-downs. They recorded their progress in a register book at a lean-to. At last, a maintainer wrote

Hikers at the Trail's northern terminus on Mount Katahdin.

During the 1960s and 70s, volunteers realized that their work alone could not keep the Appalachian Trail alive. By that time, the Trail was being lost: threatened by roads, suburban development and vacation homes. The passage by Congress of the National Trails System Act saved it.

"The federal government stepped in, purchasing land to create a protected corridor for the length of the trail," reports Pam Underhill, the National Park Service Appalachian Trail park manager. During this critical time, a strong alliance was forged between volunteers and government. "The understanding was developed that the federal government should do for the trail only that which the volunteers can't do," says Underhill. This principle of volunteer stewardship backed by government now guides the cooperative management of all national historic and scenic trails.

"Today, the Appalachian Trail is our flagship national trail," Underhill asserts, "but it's not the epic quality of the AT that impresses me the most. It's

back and asked if they wanted to join the Appalachian Trail Conference. Field laughs, "We said, 'sure,' but what was the Appalachian Trail?"

Over the next 40 years, Field learned more about the trail, rising through its volunteer ranks. In 1996 he was elected Chair of the Appalachian Trail Conference Board of Directors—the pathway's volunteer governing body. "Somewhere in the midst of it all, I decided this is what I was going to do, beside my job and family, to make a difference in the world," he says.

A Short History of Long Trails

First-time Appalachian Trail walkers often imagine this Maine-to-Georgia trail to be a primitive Indian footpath. In fact, it is an artifact of our industrial age.

The "AT," and in a sense, all national trails, arose from the mind of regional planner Benton MacKaye, who proposed the building of the Appalachian Trail in 1921. Not much later, in 1932, Clinton Clarke proposed the Pacific Crest Trail. Also in the 1930s, Oregon Trail pioneer Ezra Meeker retraced that route calling for its commemoration and protection.

Grassroots action eventually turned to government action. In 1945, Dan Hoch, an AT hiker and Pennsylvania Congressman, proposed a bill to create a "national system of foot trails." His bill failed.

In 1965, Wisconsin Senator Gaylord Nelson introduced legislation to protect the Appalachian Trail, and he led the successful effort for passage of the National Trails System Act in 1968.

"We can and should have an abundance of trails for walking, cycling and horseback riding, in and close to our cities," President Johnson said, declaring his support for the bill. "[And] in the backcountry, we need to copy the great Appalachian Trail in all parts of America."

When the National Trails System Act was signed into law, the Appalachian and Pacific Crest National Scenic Trails became the first two trails so designated. A 1978 amendment created the national historic trail category.

Today, Benton MacKaye's dream unfolds on 20 national trails. His emphasis on volunteer labor, on "an exhilarating pursuit in common," on citizen love and stewardship for trails remains a guiding force.

the devotion of people at the local level focusing on their individual parts of the trail."

Pam recently joined Field and other volunteers on Saddleback Mountain in Maine. At the time, the peak was one of the last sections of the AT still not permanently protected and a spot whose wildness was threatened by ski resort expansion. "It was so achingly beautiful on that mountaintop, looking out over a natural landscape extending to every horizon," recalls Underhill. "I found myself wanting to bring everyone I've ever cared about to that part of the trail to see what I had seen and feel what I had felt. What a special place this is."

Pacific Crest National Scenic Trail

Canada to Mexico Afoot and on Horseback

"SPIRITUALITY GROWS out of challenge," Leslie Croot muses. "And I've had no experience in my life that has been a greater challenge, a greater test to my character, tenacity, physical ability and especially my patience." This young woman is referring to her 2,650-mile journey along the Pacific Crest National Scenic Trail (PCNST), a path that links three countries— Mexico, the U.S. and Canada—and runs the length of California, Oregon and Washington.

It would be hard to surpass the PCNST for sheer extremes of terrain and climate, flora and fauna. Where it crosses the Columbia River Gorge, the path approaches sea level, while in the

Society, cars, jobs: people tell you this is the "real world." But in terms of the intensity of environment and the lessons it teaches, I think the Trail may be the only "Real World." I feel privileged to have experienced it.

Leslie Croot, PCT thru-hiker

high Sierra, it tops 13,180 feet. In the Mojave Desert, temperatures rise to 140° F, while winter readings in the Sierra Nevada mountains plunge below zero. In the Cascade Range, more than 50 feet of snow may fall. "There is no other trail that I know with a greater range of experience," says Alan Young, thru-hiker and recent president of the Pacific Crest Trail Association.

Many people view the PCNST as the companion trail to the Appalachian Trail—both were conceived at about the same time, run north and south along mountaintops and are managed by effective private-public partnerships. But that's where the similarity ends. Unlike the AT, the PCNST is both a footpath and horseback trail. It offers a chance to climb and roam well over two miles high and to enjoy some of the most remote backcountry in America. Walkers and riders may have to endure thirst and searing sun in the desert, risk fierce thunderstorms and even avalanches above treeline. But they will tell you that the rewards of the scenery far outweigh the dangers and discomforts.

The PCNST is a dramatic backcountry trail, boasting views of Mount Whitney, Mount Shasta and Mount Hood—some of the highest peaks in North America. "We could watch the mountains looming ahead for days on end as we approached," Leslie Croot recalls.

Sagebrush and spiny Joshua trees punctuate the dry southern portions of the trail. Lush forests of Sitka spruce and Pacific silver fir grace the rainy north. The PCNST traverses bone-dry washes, subalpine meadows ablaze with wildflowers, glacier-carved cirques and the snowy slopes of active volcanoes. Jackrabbits and marmots are common sights. Grizzly bear and mountain lion are present but elusive.

© LEE TERKELSEN

The PCNST passes through 19 major canyons, touches the shores of over a hundred lakes and crosses 57 mountain passes. It also intersects with five other national trails: hikers and riders ascend the same passes through which California and Oregon-bound wagoneers ventured 150 years ago. They descend into the Columbia River Gorge, boated by Lewis and Clark.

Portions of the trail were born in the 1920s when Fred Cleator of the USDA Forest Service built a skyline trail in the mountains of Oregon and Washington.

The California section developed more slowly. Californian Clinton C. Clarke first proposed a border-to-border trail in 1932. He gave three reasons for the Pacific Crest Trail. It would "get away from the honk of the auto horn or the smell of the hot dog,"

encourage "expeditions of adventure and romance," and "lead people back to a simpler and more natural life and arouse a love of nature and the outdoors."

Though the Trail remained unfinished for many years, Clarke proved that a hike along the mountainous western spine of America was possible. The first thru-hike along the trail was made, not by mountaineers, but by teenage boys. YMCA relay teams covered the 2,600 miles in four summers, arriving in Canada in 1938.

> The PCT provides a fantastic physical and mental challenge. You meet wonderful characters. It had as much effect on me as four years of college.
>
> *Alan Young, PCT thru-hiker*

The Forest Service continued building, blazing and maintaining the trail. In 1968, the National Trails System Act revitalized their work. Congress named the PCNST, along with the Appalachian Trail, as the first two national scenic trails. In 1977, the Pacific Crest Trail Association—the Trail's volunteer support organization—was formed.

Today, the PCNST links vast public lands: eight national parks and monuments, five state parks, 24 national forests, 32 national wilderness areas and four Bureau of Land Management districts.

Like all national trails, the PCNST faces challenges in the new century. "As federal budgets tighten, volunteers play an increasingly important role in maintenance," reports Alan Young. A recent membership drive has swelled PCTA members from 500 to more than

3,000 members, with 5,000 set as the organization's next goal. Volunteers actively maintain large sections of trail.

"We now do 20,000 hours of trail work per year," says Young. "Of course, we rely on the Forest Service and Bureau of Land Management for all the heavy lifting." So remote is the PCNST that crews are sometimes helicoptered into work sites.

"We're approaching Congress for funding to finish protecting the trail corridor and to preserve areas threatened by encroachment," Young adds. Three hundred miles of PCNST still cross private lands or run along public roads. The PCTA is also working to build community support with its "Trail Town" and "Adopt a Trail" programs. The group has just completed a massive two-year inventory and assessment of all the private land crossings and has proposed a $50 million, ten-year effort to secure a corridor to protect both the trail and its users from urban and commercial threats.

"I get a very warm feeling from this

trail," Alan Young confides. "It's a place to sit down at the end of the day, make a pot of coffee and find out where you've been and where you're going. It's a place that sort of wraps its arms around you and says 'welcome!' It's a great adventure."

Continental Divide National Scenic Trail

Journey Along America's Backbone

IN THE SUMMER OF 1996, the alpine ridges, dark conifer forests and desert basins of the Continental Divide National Scenic Trail (CDT) suddenly came alive with human voices. Five hundred enthusiastic explorers formed the 31 teams of the "Uniting Along the Divide" project. Continental Divide Trail Alliance volunteers, federal land managers and corporate sponsors joined in traversing 100-mile segments of one of America's most remote trails.

As they hiked and rode, making their trail assessments, the teams experienced some of the most beautiful scenery in North America. "We awoke to pastel sunrises and dined by the glow of vivid sunsets," wrote Mary Wolf, one of the participants. "We slept under a canopy of stars twinkling in an ebony sky."

To 19th century explorers and Western emigrants, the Great Divide was a largely impenetrable obstacle. Here, the sky-reaching ranges of the Rocky Mountains cut the nation in half. Down one side, streams rushed east to the Atlantic; down the other, waters poured west to the Pacific.

The Divide so dominates the Western landscape that the Blackfoot Indians called it the "center of the world." For today's outdoor adventurer it is one of the most challenging of destinations. Mile for mile, the Continental Divide Trail is among America's wildest national scenic trails. One thousand of its 3,100 miles have yet to be completed. A map and compass are essential for navigating the approximate route of a third of this hiking and equestrian trail.

The CDT is mostly a high-country pathway, almost entirely stitched together from federal and state lands. In the south, it begins at Antelope Wells on the Mexican border, called the "loneliest border station of the

> Whatever success we have on the CDT or any long-distance trail will be as a result of the volunteers that help build and maintain them.
>
> *Steve Deitemeyer, U.S. Forest Service Rocky Mountain Region director of recreation and public service*

U.S. Customs Service." In New Mexico, the trail passes through cattle ranches, volcanic badlands, barren desert and forested mountains. Cactus and mesquite, pronghorns and rattlesnakes give way to high-country ponderosa pine and Douglas fir.

In Colorado, the trail hugs the high-altitude Divide, although it descends to touch the headwaters of the Rio Grande, Platte, Colorado and Arkansas rivers. Most of the trail in this state is now marked.

In Wyoming, the CDT passes near gold mines and ghost towns and crosses the historic route of western emigrants at South Pass. This is a land made spectacular by its granite peaks, glaciers and Yellowstone geysers.

The CDT skirts snowy summits, alpine lakes and thundering waterfalls in Montana and Idaho. One landmark, the Chinese Wall, is a thousand-foot-high limestone escarpment embedded with half-billion-year-old sea fossils. The Trail descends to its lowest point at 4,200 feet, ending just north of the Canadian border in the Waterton-Glacier Peace Park.

One of the first CDT advocates was

Mt. Massive Wilderness, Colorado ©JOHN FIELDER

© JOHN FIELDER

South San Juan Wilderness, Colorado

trail; the USDA Forest Service was named federal trail administrator. In the following years, Jim's CDT Society published guidebooks for what he called a "silent trail"; this Continental Divide Trail wilderness experience came largely without the amenities of blazes or shelters.

Lacking a large volunteer base and with no federal funding, CDT construction was slow. Then, in 1995 the Continental Divide Trail Alliance was formed, with Bruce and Paula Ward as co-directors. "We wanted to make the CDT real, involve the public and build a nonprofit organization modeled after the Appalachian Trail Conference," says Bruce Ward. "The downsizing of federal government budgets demanded that we develop our own constituency and muster volunteer resources to build and maintain the trail.

Jim Wolf, from Baltimore, Maryland. "In 1973 I began to believe in the feasibility of a Continental Divide Trail," Wolf remembers. "I set out to hike it, with the idea of developing a series of guidebooks." Unknown to Jim Wolf, the federal government was also studying the possibilities for such a trail.

In 1978, Congress designated the Continental Divide Trail as the third great north-to-south national scenic

"We want the CDT to be more than a linear path for thru-hikers," says Ward. "We see it as a way to draw attention to important issues on public lands. In the past, grazing, logging and mining were the integral components

Completing and protecting the Continental Divide Trail will guarantee that our children—your children—will always have somewhere wild to go. But setting aside the 3,100 miles of trail is not something we can do alone. It takes a team of volunteers and donors willing to invest in the future of this national treasure.

Steve Fausel, CDT Alliance national spokesman

of Western land management. Now, we're increasing the value of recreation in the consciousness of land managers and the public. We think we can truly make a difference and create a legacy for generations to come."

Between 1996 and 1998, the CDT Alliance contributed 56,000 hours of volunteer labor to the trail project. The group also lobbied successfully for the appropriation of $1.5 million for CDT construction. They've worked hard to turn trail neighbors into trail supporters. The "Uniting Along the Divide" and "Adopt-A-Trail" programs are two examples of the group's continuing success.

"The CDT is a big trail," declares Steve Deitemeyer, Forest Service director of recreation and public service for the Rocky Mountain Region. "There's no way we'll have 3,100 miles of continuity unless people work together to get it done. It's the Forest Service role to coordinate with our volunteer groups to complete the trail and share our public lands. Ultimately, the CDT will connect special places, unique geology, ecosystems and communities. The trail experience will bind and bond us all to the land."

North Country National Scenic Trail

Adventure Just Beyond Your Own Back Door

THE RESTLESS WAVES OF Lake Superior have carved Pictured Rocks National Lakeshore into a succession of spectacular scenes. Sandstone bluffs are endlessly reshaped by wind and water into fantastic turrets, pinnacles and arches. Brooks wander to the edge of the 200-foot escarpment and topple in white sheets and ribbons into the lake below.

This inspiring spot on Michigan's Upper Peninsula is one of many "jewels" to be found along the North Country National Scenic Trail (NCNST). The path is among the most varied of national scenic trails, traversing the rural landscape of seven

Indian Head, Pictured Rocks National Lakeshore, Michigan

northern states and exploring outstanding natural, recreational, historical and cultural sites. It encompasses wilderness and farmland, 19th century canal towpaths and railroad beds. It passes 18th century trading posts, Revolutionary War forts, historic villages, taverns and inns.

Despite this rich diversity, the NCNST remains relatively unknown. While hundreds of walkers thru-hike the Appalachian Trail every year, only a handful of people are known to have traveled the NCNST end to end. "One of the delights of the North Country Trail is that it is a trail awaiting discovery," claims Wes Boyd, guidebook author and former editor of the North Country Trail Association's magazine, *The North Star*.

The North Country Trail is an immense work in progress. When designated by Congress in 1980, it was to be 3,200 miles long. Over the years, the route has been mapped and remapped. As envisioned by many today, the NCNST will be the longest national scenic trail, snaking across 4,600 miles, linking parks and communities from New York to North Dakota.

Its eastern terminus is on New York's Lake Champlain at Crown Point, a French and Indian War

View from the Trail: farmland in upstate New York

stronghold. The route leads west into the great silences of Adirondack Mountain boreal forest. The trail plays tag with New York's Finger Lakes, probes Pennsylvania's Allegheny Plateau, makes a deep loop south into Ohio farm country, then shoots north into Michigan's Lower Peninsula.

> We're not working to create just any neighborhood trail; we're creating one of the great trails of our nation.
>
> *Tom Gilbert, Superintendent,*
> *North Country National Scenic Trail*

The NCNST crosses the Straits of Mackinac, and enters some of its wildest terrain on Michigan's Upper Peninsula. Wisconsin forest gives way to Minnesota lake country. Finally, the trail enters open prairie and achieves its western terminus in the Big Sky Country of central North Dakota. The NCNST ends where it meets the

The Power of Partnerships

The National Trails System is an extraordinary web of public and private partnerships, without which none of the trails could exist. Each of the 22 trails is administered by a federal agency in partnership with at least one volunteer-based nonprofit association.

The administering government agency is responsible for coordinating actions along the trail, including trail protection, markings and signs, compliance and technical assistance for volunteers, state and local governments and landowners. The National Park Service currently administers 17 national trails, the USDA Forest Service four and the Bureau of Land Management two trails.

Volunteer partners form the backbone of each national trail and perform much on-the-ground work. Volunteers wade waist deep in swamps to build the Florida Trail; they negotiate trail easements on the Ice Age Trail; they manage a scholarly library on the California Trail; and they monitor endangered species along the Appalachian Trail.

The ultimate beneficiary of this marriage between public and private sectors is the American public. Volunteers donate thousands of hours in expertise and physical labor to the trails. "They are a precious resource," says National Park Service Appalachian Trail Manager Pam Underhill. "No matter how high we raise the bar, the volunteers just keep jumping over it."

Volunteers likewise recognize the indispensable role government partners play. "Without our federal administrator," says Mike Dahl, Vice President of the Overmountain Victory Trail Association, "we would have recently lost one of our most important historical sites to a four-lane highway."

Missouri River and the Lewis and Clark National Historic Trail.

The USDA Forest Service first proposed the NCNST in 1965. "It was to link nine national forests in seven states," recalls Lance Feild, a founder of the North Country Trail Association. "The idea was to add a much-needed east-west trail to the National Trails System. We also wanted people in the central U.S. to be able to hike a long-distance trail without driving a thousand miles to the Appalachian or Pacific Crest Trails."

In 1975, an approximate route was agreed to by federal and state officials and volunteers. Congress designated the NCNST a national scenic trail in 1980, with the National Park Service chosen as federal administrator. The North Country Trail Association (NCTA), the volunteer partner, was chartered in 1981. A government and volunteer alliance placed nearly a third of the trail on the ground, most of it on public lands, by 1995.

"Now, we've turned a corner," says Bob Papp, executive director of the NCTA. "In the early days, the trail was driven by a small, active volunteer core, working closely with public land managers. But the remaining unfinished sections will be mostly on private lands. Today, to be successful, we need a much broader base of support. We need local people to talk to township boards and meet with local landowners." The NCTA is cultivating a powerful grassroots organization. In four recent years, it grew from just four to 21 chapters.

Routing nearly 2,500 miles of trail across private land sounds daunting, but local chapters are proving it can be done. "In a single year, Michigan's Chief Noonday Chapter built 20 miles of trail on private property without requiring any land acquisition," Papp says. Government partners are also actively moving to put the trail on the ground. In 1998, the U.S. Bureau of Reclamation and Garrison Diversion Conservancy District in North Dakota teamed up to build 115 miles of NCNST along the New Rockford and McClusky Canals.

The North Country Trail has also grown by co-aligning its new miles with regional trails already in place. The Finger Lakes Trail in New York, Buckeye and Cannonball Trails in Ohio and Superior Hiking Trail in Minnesota, for example, have all joined in partnerships with the NCTA to manage the NCNST.

"A couple hundred miles of the Finger Lakes Trail were ready-made for

Old Man's Cave section of the North Country Trail, Ohio

the NCNST," says Stephanie Spittal, former president of the Finger Lakes Trail Conference. The union benefits everyone: the North Country Trail adds to its mileage, while the regional trails gain visibility and become eligible for National Park Service funding and support.

"One of our biggest challenges remains public awareness," Bob Papp says. "There are people who live five miles away from the North Country Trail who probably are better informed about the Appalachian Trail. We recognize that the more public awareness we create, the greater our constituency will be and the more enthusiastic our support will become."

Florida National Scenic Trail

Trekking the Subtropics Step by Step

THE FLORIDA TRAIL penetrates one of the state's most remote backcountry regions along the banks of the Kissimmee River. Oak and sable palm hammocks and open prairie line the river's shore. Live oaks drip with Spanish moss. Thickets harbor hawk and owl, fox and bobcat, feral hog and armadillo.

"Looking out over the river floodplain is almost like looking into the African veldt," says Florida Trail Association former Vice President for Trails Fred Schiller. "I've seen Audubon's caracara, great blue herons, snowy egrets and sandhill cranes. They're even trying to reestablish whooping cranes out there."

Hiking? Backcountry? Florida? The words don't go together in many people's minds. But the 5,300-member Florida Trail Association (FTA) will tell you differently. The mountain-free Sunshine State is among the nation's richest in biodiversity. The Florida Trail experience boasts bald cypress, laurel oak, sable palms, burrowing owls, red-cockaded woodpeckers, indigo snakes and gopher tortoises—flora and fauna found along no other national scenic trail.

When finished, the Florida National Scenic Trail (FNST) will traverse 1,300 miles of subtropical and tropical habitat. Traveling from west to east and north to south, the Trail starts in the Florida Panhandle at Gulf Islands National Seashore. Here the path passes along white sand beaches and dunes edging the Gulf of Mexico. In Eglin Air Force Base, it crosses clear, sand-bottomed creeks in the folds of rolling hills covered in long leaf and sand pine forests.

The Trail's longest continuous segment extends through the Apalachicola National Forest and the St. Marks National Wildlife Refuge. In the national forest, it passes through the 23,000-acre Bradwell Bay Wilderness

> I'm saddened by the many Americans who settle into couches with their remotes. Sooner or later people will discover the joys of walking. The National Trails System will be there when they do.
>
> *Jim Kern, founder, FTA*

with its titi thickets, deep gum swamps, virgin pine and cypress forests. The national wildlife refuge is home to more than 300 bird species and remnant Confederate salt works. It follows limestone bluffs along the Suwannee River and enters the pine flatwoods of Osceola National Forest. In Ocala National Forest it pulls up beside wet prairies, sinkholes, ponds, rivers and bubbling freshwater springs.

From Ocala southward, the trail splits in two, passing through the populous central section of the state. The eastern route is mostly complete. Skirting Orlando, it follows newly cut hiking trail along creeks and lakeshores. It parallels tree-lined dikes and old railroad grades through hardwood swamps, pine flatlands, open pastures, cypress-dotted prairie and scrub oak forest. A more remote western trail route passes through the Cross Florida Greenway and along the Withlacoochee River.

The FNST circles 110 miles around

Buffer Trail, central Florida ©JUDY ELSEROAD

Lake Okeechobee on the Hoover Dike, built by the U.S. Army Corps of Engineers. The 30-foot-high levee offers views of the vast lake, plus surrounding cattle ranches and sugarcane fields. The Florida Trail ends in Big Cypress National Preserve, amid sawgrass marsh dotted by tropical hammocks of sabal palm. Orchids and

bromeliads hang on cypress trees like colorful ornaments. This wild country is the last refuge of the Florida panther.

Wildlife photographer and real estate broker Jim Kern first envisioned the Florida Trail in 1964. Dubious officials told him no one would ever come to pancake-flat Florida to hike. Kern set out to prove them wrong, launching the Florida Trail Association and making a 160-mile backpacking trip down the center of the state.

While Kern earned media coverage and an initial swell of public interest, false starts nearly derailed the trail. "In the early '70s we sought preservation of the right-of-way by going to the Florida legislature and asking them to declare eminent domain for the Florida Trail," Kern says, chuckling at his naivete. "We were so wet behind the ears. We got slaughtered! The timber, cattle and orange industries made sure our plan went nowhere."

But the grassroots trail-building effort flourished. With virtually no federal or state money, the FTA volunteers built the trail mile by mile. In 1986 Congress designated the Florida Trail as a national scenic trail, recognizing the FTA as "one of the most effective citizen trail developing and maintaining organizations in the country." The USDA Forest Service serves as the trail's federal administrator.

Today, more than 660 miles of the orange-blazed Florida Trail are on the ground, with another 330 miles proposed. FTA volunteers also built and maintain 300 miles of loop trails complementing the FNST. "We have a vigorous volunteer effort underway, with 16 regional chapters, all active and excited about the trail," says Fred Schiller.

"You can imagine how difficult it is to build and maintain a tropical trail. Things grow fast here," Schiller

Above: hooded pitcher plant, which blooms in bogs, pinelands and marshes along the FNST. Right: hikers on a log bridge with cable hand-hold.

© JUDY ELSEROAD

©FLORIDA TRAIL ASSOCIATION

explains. Florida gets 50 to 65 inches of rain per year, watering a bumper crop of fast-growing grasses, trees, tangled vines and spiny palmetto. "Our volunteers work from fall to spring, in cool, dry weather, when insect populations are low. They trim, lop and mow the treadway and repaint blazes." Constructing new trail is equally challenging. Volunteers sometimes wade waist-deep through swamps, building bridges and boardwalk. FTA members volunteer more than 40,000 hours annually.

Today, the FNST is managed cooperatively by the USDA Forest Service and the FTA, in partnership with federal and state parks and forests and private landowners.

While the path continues to grow in length, it remains under-funded and only partially protected. The FNST is currently about half complete, with nearly all its miles on public lands. Exploding development threatens the trail's completion. As with several other national trails, funding for land protection of the corridor has not been adequate to finish the job.

"The trail will be completed. That's inevitable," declares an optimistic Jim Kern. "But the longer we wait, the more subdivisions pop up, and the more the natural lines of the trail corridor will be jeopardized. Floridians must get behind their trail and preserve the corridor. Then we can take a deep sigh of relief."

Selma to Montgomery National Historic Trail

Retracing the Footsteps of America's Civil Rights Movement

AT JUST 54 MILES, the Selma to Montgomery route is the shortest of the national historic trails, but it is long on significance. The events that occurred on the roads linking these Alabama cities are vividly etched in living memory.

"When I got to Selma I found a children's movement in full swing," relates James Webb, a 17-year-old civil rights worker in 1965. "Kids were organizing to get the right to vote for their parents. Martin Luther King sent me to Selma, along with others, to train teenagers in nonviolent resistance: 'satyagraha,' soul force, what Gandhi used in South Africa and India."

The Selma youths faced an entrenched, sometimes violent foe. While post-Civil War constitutional amendments granted black Americans the legal right to vote, Southern white conservatives denied that right. Illegal poll taxes, fraudulent literacy tests, beatings, burnings, bombings and murder kept blacks disenfranchised. In Lowndes County, outside Selma, for example, nearly 80 percent of the population was African-American, but not one among them dared vote.

"Fear opened our eyes bright," recalls Betty Fikes, a Selma teenager in 1965 and a runner for SNCC (the Student Non-Violent Coordinating Committee). "There was so much injustice over the land. We were ready to fight. We didn't know we were making history. Like other children my age, I was doing what I had to do."

The voters' rights march from Selma to Montgomery was actually three marches. The first was spontaneously organized in memory of Jimmie Lee Jackson, an African-American voters' rights protestor shot to death by Alabama state troopers in February 1965.

Five hundred marchers gathered at Brown Chapel African Methodist Episcopal Church on March 7. Led by Hosea Williams and John Lewis, they headed toward Montgomery to confront segregationist Governor George Wallace.

"We didn't understand why there were no police harassing us that day. It was very unusual," remembers Webb. On the far side of the Edmund Pettus

Bridge, which carries Highway 80 from Selma's downtown over the Alabama River, the marchers found out why. "In front of us was a sea of Alabama state troopers. They put on gas masks and started firing tear gas at us. They beat and drove us back across the bridge. People all around me were kneeling and praying and getting struck."

Betty Fikes anxiously awaited news of the march on the steps of Brown Chapel. "There was a calmness, a stillness in the air. I felt sure something was about to happen," she recalls. "Then the ground was shaking like an earthquake. People were screaming, running for their lives from police deputies on horseback with billy clubs." At that moment, a Biblical quote swept into Betty's mind: "God so loved the world that He sent His only begotten Son . . ." Where was God now, she wondered.

That night, scenes from the Bloody Sunday march were broadcast on national television. Many Americans were outraged at the fierce unprovoked attack by lawmen on nonviolent marchers. "People just came to Selma without being asked," says Webb of the spontaneous groundswell that followed. "We had a song: 'They comin' by bus, by airplane too, they'd walk if ya asked them to! O Wallace, you never can jail us all, segregation's bound to fall!'"

Dr. Martin Luther King, Jr., came to Selma to lead the second march. This "Turn around Tuesday" repeated

Top to bottom: Brown Chapel Church, Bloody Sunday, Edmund Pettus Bridge

The third march, led by Martin Luther King, Jr., took place on March 21, 1965, just 18 days after Bloody Sunday.

the Bloody Sunday route to the far side of the Pettus Bridge. King and his followers stopped there, respecting a federal court order delaying a complete Selma to Montgomery march. That evening in Selma, visiting Unitarian minister James Reeb was beaten to death by white segregationists.

On March 15, President Johnson introduced the National Voting Rights bill to Congress and recognized the Selma marchers: "Their cause must be our cause, too. Because it is not just Negroes, but really it's all of us who must overcome the crippling legacy of

> Confrontation of good and evil, compressed in the tiny community of Selma, generated the massive power to turn the whole Nation to a new course.
>
> *Dr. Martin Luther King, Jr.*

bigotry and injustice. And we shall overcome."

With the lifting of the court order, a third march was launched, this time under the protection of the National Guard. The marchers left Brown Chapel on March 21, just 18 days after Bloody Sunday.

"The danger we were in never entered our minds," says Webb. "On our way to Montgomery, we weren't afraid of state police or Wallace. We knew we had cracked a chink in the enemy's armor. We had read Thomas Paine. If there had to be war, let it be in our day so we could be free!"

Only 300 made the entire walk; the number was limited by the courts. Led by Martin Luther King, Jr., they camped in fields near U.S. Highway 80. When the protestors entered Montgomery on March 25, their number swelled to an estimated 25,000. Dr. King addressed the crowd from a flatbed truck at the Capitol steps, the same spot at which Jefferson Davis had been inaugurated. It was the largest civil rights march to ever take place in the South.

That night, in the day's triumphant aftermath, Viola Liuzzo—who had driven alone from Detroit to assist in the protest—was murdered by Ku Klux Klansmen. Less than five months later, President Johnson signed the Voting Rights Act into law, and blacks throughout the South streamed into courthouses to register to vote. Southern political life was forever changed.

Challenges for a New Millennium

A growing population and a quickening pace of change pose formidable challenges to the National Trails System. Today's trail-makers must constantly balance the preservation of treadway, natural and cultural resources, against the public need for recreation.

Fame brings problems to some national trails. Crowding on the Appalachian Trail threatens the wilderness experience. Managers worry about the intense human pressures placed upon primitive shelter and sanitation systems and on the survivability of rare and endangered species.

Lack of public awareness works against other trails. In the past, historic wagon ruts on the Oregon Trail were often plowed under or paved over simply because people were not aware of their existence or their value.

The vast scope of the National Trails System—its thousands of miles of narrow corridor, combined with limited staffing and tiny operating budgets—demands innovative problem solving.

In the new century, sophisticated satellite global positioning systems and electronic mapping will help managers map corridors and pinpoint fragile resources. Computerized databases will allow the tracking of trail conditions, ownership, resource conditions and land use threats. Hundreds of trail websites already introduce trails to a public hungry for recreation.

The more our modern lifestyle threatens our natural and cultural heritage, the more important the National Trails System may become. The national trails are a gateway to authenticity.

"Our kids aren't going to learn about the outdoors from a car window," Congressman Gaylord Nelson once declared. "They have to see our natural surroundings as the first settlers did to really appreciate this wonderful country."

In 1996, Congress designated the Selma to Montgomery March route as a national historic trail. The bill was sponsored by Congressman John Lewis, co-leader of the Bloody Sunday march. At the same time, the U.S. Department of Transportation recognized the route as an All-American Road.

"It's not only a national trail, but an international trail," James Webb maintains. "I've met youth in the jungles of South Africa and Zimbabwe, and they've shown me smuggled Selma to Montgomery videotapes. The March inspires the youth of revolutionary freedom movements in Namibia, China and around the world."

Appendix

National Trails System Contacts

(in alphabetical order, by trail)

APPALACHIAN NATIONAL SCENIC TRAIL
Appalachian Trail Conference   Brian Fitzgerald, Chair
P.O. Box 807, Harpers Ferry, WV 25425   David Startzell, Exec. Dir.
(304) 535-6331;   FAX (304) 535-2667
www.appalachiantrail.org/

NPS Appalachian National Scenic Trail Office
Harpers Ferry Center   Pam Underhill, Park Manager
Harpers Ferry, WV 25425
(304) 535-6278;   FAX (304) 535-6270
www.nps.gov/appa

CALIFORNIA NATIONAL HISTORIC TRAIL
Oregon-California Trails Association   Randy Wagner, President
P.O. Box 1019, Independence, MO 64051-0519   Kathy Conway, Exec. Director
(816) 252-2276;   FAX (816) 836-0989
www.OCTA-trails.org

NPS Long-Distance Trails Office, Salt Lake City
324 S. State St., P.O. Box 45155   Jere Krakow, Superintendent
Salt Lake City, UT 84145-0155
(801) 539-4095; FAX (801) 539-4098
www.nps.gov/cali/

CONTINENTAL DIVIDE NATIONAL SCENIC TRAIL
Continental Divide Trail Alliance   Bruce and Paula Ward
P.O. Box 628, Pine, CO 80470
(303) 838-3760;   FAX (303) 838-3960
www.CDTrail.org

Continental Divide Trail Society
3704 N. Charles St., #601, Baltimore, MD 21218-2300
(410) 235-9610
www.gorp.com/cdts/

Jim Wolf

USDA-FS Rocky Mountain Regional Office
740 Simms, Golden, CO 80401
(303) 275-5045; FAX (303) 275-5366

Greg Warren

FLORIDA NATIONAL SCENIC TRAIL
Florida Trail Association
P.O. Box 13708, Gainesville, FL 32604
(352) 378-8823; (800) 343-1882
FAX (352) 378-4550
www.florida-trail.org/

Deborah Stewart-Kent, Pres.

USDA-FS, National Forests in Florida
325 John Knox Rd., #F-100
Tallahassee, FL 32303
(850) 942-9376; FAX (850) 942-9305

Kent Wimmer, FTA Liaison

ICE AGE NATIONAL SCENIC TRAIL
Ice Age Park and Trail Foundation, Inc.
207 E. Buffalo St., #515,
Milwaukee, WI 53202-5712
(414) 278-8518; FAX (414) 278-8665
www.iceagetrail.org/

Tom Drought, President
Christine Thisted, Exec. Director

NPS Ice Age National Scenic Trail
700 Rayovac Drive, Suite 100
Madison, WI 53711
(608) 441-5610; FAX (608) 441-5615
www.nps.gov/iatr

Tom Gilbert, Superintendent
Pam Schuler, Trail Manager

IDITAROD NATIONAL HISTORIC TRAIL
Iditarod National Historic Trail Inc.
P.O. Box 2323, Seward, AK 99664
(907) 443-2798

Leo Rasmussen, President

BLM Anchorage District
6881 Abbott Loop Road, Anchorage, AK 99507
(907) 267-1207; FAX (907) 267-1267
www.anchorage.ak.blm.gov/inhthome.html

Mike Zaidlicz

JUAN BAUTISTA DE ANZA NATIONAL HISTORIC TRAIL

Amigos de Anza   Peter Cole, President
c/o 1350 Castle Rock Road
Walnut Canyon, CA 94598
(510) 926-1081
www.therapure.com/anza-trail/

Juan Bautista de Anza NHT
c/o NPS Pacific-Great Basin Office   Meredith Kaplan, Superintendent
1111 Jackson Street, #700
Oakland, CA 94607
(510) 817–1438; FAX (510) 817–1505
www.nps.gov/juba/ or http://anza.uoregon.edu

LEWIS AND CLARK NATIONAL HISTORIC TRAIL

Lewis and Clark Trail Heritage Foundation, Inc.   Jane Henley, President
P.O. Box 3434, Great Falls, MT 59403   Cari Carns, Executive Director
(406) 454-1234; FAX (406) 454-0448
www.lewisandclark.org

National Council for the Lewis and Clark Bicentennial
Lewis and Clark College   David Borlaug, President
0615 SW Palatine Hill Road   Michelle Bussard, Exec. Dir.
Portland, OR 97219
(503) 768-7995/6 or (888) 999-1803; FAX (530) 768-7994
www.lewisandclark200.org or www.lewis-clark.org

NPS Lewis and Clark National Historic Trail
1709 Jackson St.   Gerard Baker, Superintendent
Omaha, NE 68102
(402) 514-9311; FAX (402) 827-9108

MORMON PIONEER NATIONAL HISTORIC TRAIL

Mormon Trails Association   Gar Elison, President
300 S. Rio Grande, Salt Lake City, UT 84101
www.history.utah.org/partners/mta

NPS Long-Distance Trails Office, SLC
324 S. State St., P.O. Box 45155   Jere Krakow, Superintendent
Salt Lake City, UT 84145-0155
(801) 539-4095; FAX (801) 539-4098
www.nps.gov/mopi

NATCHEZ TRACE NATIONAL SCENIC TRAIL

Natchez Trace Trail Conference, Inc.　　　　Hillary Wright, President
c/o 114 N. Meadows Pl., Jackson, MS 39211

Superintendent, Natchez Trace Parkway
2680 Natchez Trace Parkway　　　　Jackie Henman, Park Trail Coordinator
Tupelo, MS 38801
(662) 680-4014;　FAX (662) 680-4034
www.nps.gov/natt/

NEZ PERCE (NEE-ME-POO) NATIONAL HISTORIC TRAIL

Nez Perce National Historic Trail Foundation　　　　Nick Hudson, President
P.O. Box 1939, Lewiston, ID 83501　　　Brian McCormack, Vice-President
www.public.iastate.edu/~sfr/npnhtf/npnhtf.html

c/o Clearwater National Forest
12730 Highway 12　　　　　　　　　　　　　Sandi McFarland
Orofino, ID 83544
(208) 476-8334; FAX (208) 476-8329

NORTH COUNTRY NATIONAL SCENIC TRAIL

North Country Trail Association　　　　　Gaylord Yost, President
229 E. Main St.　　　　　　　　　Bob Papp, Executive Director
Lowell, MI 49331
(616) 897-5987;　FAX (616) 897-6605
www.northcountrytrail.org/

NPS North Country National Scenic Trail
700 Rayovac Drive, Suite 100　　　　Tom Gilbert, Superintendent
Madison, WI 53711　　　　　　　Fred Szarka, Trail Manager
(608) 441-5610;　FAX (608) 441-5615
www.nps.gov/noco

OREGON NATIONAL HISTORIC TRAIL

Oregon-California Trails Association　　　　David Welch, President
P.O. Box 1019　　　　　　　Cathy Conway, Exec. Director
Independence, MO 64051-0519
(816) 252-2276;　FAX (816) 836-0989
www.OCTA-trails.org

NPS Long-Distance Trails Office, Salt Lake City
324 S. State St., P.O. Box 45155
Salt Lake City, UT 84145-0155
(801) 539-4095; FAX (801) 539-4098
www.nps.gov/oreg

Jere Krakow, Superintendent

OVERMOUNTAIN VICTORY NATIONAL HISTORIC TRAIL
Overmountain Victory Trail Association
c/o Sycamore Shoals State Historic Area
1651 West Elk Avenue, Elizabethton, TN 37643
(615) 543-5808
www.ovta.org

Allen Ray, President

c/o Kings Mountain National Military Park
2625 Park Road
Blacksburg, SC 29702
(864) 936-7921

Paul Carson, Trail Planner

PACIFIC CREST NATIONAL SCENIC TRAIL
Pacific Crest Trail Association
5325 Elkhorn Blvd. PMB #256
Sacramento, CA 95842
(916) 349-2109; FAX (916) 349-1268
www.pcta.org/

David Foscue, President
Liz Bergeron, Ex. Dir.

USDA-FS Pacific Southwest Regional Office
1324 Club Dr., Vallejo, CA 94592
(707) 562-8970; FAX (707) 562-9055

Tim Stone

PONY EXPRESS NATIONAL HISTORIC TRAIL
National Pony Express Association
P.O. Box 236
Pollock Pines, CA 95726
www.xphomestation.com/

George Lange, President

NPS Long-Distance Trails Office, Salt Lake City
324 S. State St., P.O. Box 45155
Salt Lake City, UT 84145-0155
(801) 539-4095; FAX (801) 539-4098
www.nps.gov/poex/

Jere Krakow, Superintendent

POTOMAC HERITAGE NATIONAL SCENIC TRAIL

Potomac Heritage Partnership
1623 28th St., NW, Washington, DC 20007
(202) 338-6222;   FAX (202) 333-2887

Janice Artemel, Director

Potomac Trail Council
c/o AHS, 1422 Fenwick Lane
Silver Spring, MD 20910
www.potomactrail.org

David Lillard, President

Potomac Heritage NST
P. O. Box B,
Harpers Ferry, WV
(304) 535-4016;   FAX (304) 535-4020
www.nps.gov/pohe/

Donald Briggs, Superintendent

SANTA FE NATIONAL HISTORIC TRAIL

Santa Fe Trail Association
Santa Fe Trail Center, Rte. 3
Larned, KS 67550
(316) 285-2054
www.nmhu.edu/research/sftrail/sfta.htm

Hal Jackson, President

NPS Long-Distance Trails, Santa Fe
P.O. Box 728, Santa Fe, NM 87504-0728
(505) 988-6888;   FAX (505) 986-5214
www.nps.gov/safe/

David Gaines, Superintendent

SELMA TO MONTGOMERY NATIONAL HISTORIC TRAIL

401 Adams Avenue #424
Montgomery, AL 36103-5690
(334) 353-3858; FAX (334) 353-3749

Catherine Former, Site Manager

TRAIL OF TEARS NATIONAL HISTORIC TRAIL

Trail of Tears Association
c/o Paul Austin, American Indian Center
of Arkansas, 1100 N. University, #133
Little Rock, AR 72207
(501) 666-9032;   FAX (501) 666-5875

Jack Baker, President

NPS Long-Distance Trails, Santa Fe
P.O. Box 728, Santa Fe, NM, 87504-0728
(505) 988-6888;   FAX (505) 986-5214
www.nps.gov/fosm/history/tot/index.htm

David Gaines, Superintendent

NATIONAL AGENCIES AND ORGANIZATIONS

AMERICAN HIKING SOCIETY
1422 Fenwick Lane, Silver Spring, MD 20910   H. Neil Zimmerman, Chairman
(301) 565-6704; FAX (301) 565-6714   Mary Margaret Sloan, President
E-mail: info@americanhiking.org
www.americanhiking.org

PARTNERSHIP FOR THE NATIONAL TRAILS SYSTEM
2302 Lakeland Ave.   Gary Werner, Exec. Dir.
Madison, WI 53704
(608) 249-7870; FAX (608) 257-3513
E-mail: nattrails@aol.com

BUREAU OF LAND MANAGEMENT
6221 Box Springs Blvd.   Deb Smith
Riverside, CA 92507
(909) 697-5309
E-mail: debsmith@blm.gov

NATIONAL PARK SERVICE
National Center for Recreation and Conservation
1849 C St., NW, Washington, DC 20240   D. Thomas Ross, Assist. Dir.,
(202) 565-1200;   FAX (202) 565-1204   Steven Elkinton, Program Leader
E-mail: steve_elkinton@nps.gov

USDA-FOREST SERVICE
Dispersed Recreation Program Manager   Jim Miller
USDA-Forest Service, P.O. Box 96090, (RH&WR)
Washington, DC 20090-6090
(202) 205-1313;   FAX (202) 205-1145
E-mail: jbmiller01@fs.fed.us